Escaping Suburbia

A 1960S MERSEYSIDE CHILDHOOD

DAVID J. EVELEIGH

Foreword by Sir Neil Cossons

The History Press

First published 2019

The History Press
97 St George's Place, Cheltenham,
Gloucestershire, GL50 3QB
www.thehistorypress.co.uk

British Library Cataloguing in Publication Data.
A catalogue record for this book is available from the British Library.

ISBN 978 0 7509 9239 8

Typesetting and origination by The History Press
Printed and bound in Great Britain by TJ International Ltd

Contents

Acknowledgements

When I began this project I asked Nick Wright, with whom I had worked on two previous publications, if he could read through my draft text as it evolved, and serve as my mentor. Nick performed this task with brutal honesty: it was what I wanted. 'No one is interested in you,' he said, and I have no doubt he is right. I had to make sure that my account was not a load of senseless drivel that would appeal to no one – except me – so through the eighteen months of writing and corrections, Nick performed the role of mentor superbly. I am indebted to him. I would also like to thank Sir Neil Cossons, who read and commented on the text and provided the foreword. I also received help from many other quarters. Thus, I am grateful to my mother for checking my recollections of certain events and things. Bernard Thornley, my history teacher from Wirral Grammar School, read through the chapter on my time at the school and provided some very useful background information as well as saving me from a few factual errors. Donal Hickey from Killarney, formerly a journalist with the *Cork Examiner*, made some invaluable observations on the section on Ireland. Thanks are also due to Barbara James, granddaughter of Catherine Connor, and to Ann Evans, née Chadwick, who replied to requests for information. I must also thank some old friends and former colleagues who read through drafts of the book. So, I extend my warmest thanks to Richard Wynne Davies, Alison Farrar, John Freeman, Peter Hofford, Adrian Targett, Mel Weatherley and also Dave Ring – who is normally too busy making tea and playing golf to read anything – for their invaluable feedback. Thanks are due to National Museums Liverpool and Wirral Archives for their assistance, and I am also grateful to the Williamson Art Gallery & Museum, Birkenhead, for permission to include the two paintings by Harold Hopps of Kings Farm and Higher Bebington Mill; to Birkenhead Central Library for permission to use the illustrations on pages 20, 135, 136, 140 and 149 and to Abbey Garrad and her colleague, Tom, who ran the extra mile in making the library's photograph archive accessible. I am also grateful to C.M. Whitehouse for permission to use his photograph of locomotive 42587 on page 138. I am also very grateful to The History Press for turning my typescript into a book and to the team who worked on the project with remarkable speed and efficiency.

Finally, I need to thank my partner, Geraldine, for her patience: from the beginning she has had to put up with me talking endlessly of this project.

D.J.E.
31 March 2019

Foreword

There is a frequently quoted saying: 'If you can remember the sixties, you weren't really there', which, despite its supposed origins in California, might have applied equally to Liverpool, then riding high on the reflected glory of The Beatles and all they represented. These were the years when the American beat poet Allen Ginsberg saw Liverpool as 'The centre of the consciousness of the human universe'.

This book is the antithesis of all those sixties clichés. Here, David Eveleigh's acutely vivid observations and the reflections that emerge from them paint a very different picture: of a boyhood characterised by its essential ordinariness, set out with an engaging kindness and clarity. It is his ability to portray the everyday that makes this such a refreshing read. His is a detached yet personal portrayal of his surroundings during his boyhood years, about his home and his home life in Bebington on the Wirral peninsula in Cheshire – unquestionably not Liverpool but, crucially, Merseyside. A childhood in a three-bed 1930s semi, with an open coal fire burning Sunbright Number 2 and a table lamp made from a Mateus rosé wine bottle, reflected a familiarity invisible to most, but it is seen here as a prelude to change and all that went with emerging sixties affluence and the cupidity that was part of it. Yet his views are not about the acquisition of material things – on the contrary – but of the inescapability of the events that take place around him. Here lies the strength of this book.

He notes, and to an extent revels in, the Victorian buildings of his surroundings – if only because they are leftovers from another age, unfashionable and despised, condemned to disappear in the face of acres of new housing.

Yet the pull of aspiration and the desire for the new takes his own family and him with it into this new world, to a new house, new household goods and, crucially, a new place that is detached. That his house no longer touched its neighbour, however small the gap between them, signalled a difference that mattered long before the word affluence had been discovered. His was a loving middle class family, offering a stable boyhood and allowing David the space to reflect in comfort and with quiet surprise.

Nor are these nostalgic sentiments (although there are painful regrets as steam railway locomotives disappear), more a quiet non-judgmental succession of observations on all that went on about him. He reflects too on summer holidays: by train to North Wales, later to Ireland by plane and then in the family car, by boat to Dublin and the long drive down to the south west. These holidays were spent in hotels, again a sign of a new and real prosperity, a defining feature of sixties change. Here, in Skibbereen, on a flickering black and white television, he saw man for the first time put his foot on the moon. David Eveleigh's sixties boyhood ended with that holiday.

Neil Cossons

Introduction

It is probably true to say that I have been writing this book all my life. At least in my head and at least from the time we left my grandparents' house, my first home, in 1959. From then onwards I stored up memories of my childhood, kept diaries for some years and held on to other things, mementos of my childhood including books, toys and some of my drawings. But it was only in 2017 that I started writing. We were on holiday in Greece on the wonderfully quiet and peaceful island of Alonissos. I bought an exercise book and black biro in the newsagents in the main town, Patitiri, and with a clear head – away from the pressures of work and everyday life – and with the blue Aegean in front of me, I laid down the first 6,000 words longhand. Upon returning home I typed up my manuscript, editing and refining the text as I went, and soon completed part one, whilst at the same time sketching out a structure for the rest.

This obviously begged questions as to the purpose of the book. My shorthand for the project when talking to friends and family was my 'memoirs'. But I quickly realised that the book should not constitute a blow-by-blow account of my childhood; neither was I attempting to write a comprehensive social and cultural history of the 1960s. That has been done superbly by others. The finished book lies somewhere between the two. It is an account of one very ordinary boy growing up in the '60s, perhaps with a larger than average dose of nostalgic sentiment and interest in the past, and forms a compendium of personal experiences and observations. Some of these are trivial, personal and obvious, but they are very likely experiences shared by, or at least very similar to, those of other children from this time. The recollections of how my parents furnished their new house in 1959, how I started school, watched TV and underwent life at secondary school – in my case a state grammar school –

describe experiences that I expect many readers will identify with and will perhaps trigger recollections of their own childhood.

The book also contains my memories of how I reacted to the wider world. As a young child I had no idea that I was born on the cusp between two post-war eras: austerity and boom. Rationing had ended only in 1954, the year before I was born, and had effectively closed the period of austerity, of make do and mend, utility and frugality, but within three or four years the floodgates of the boom years opened. Utility was replaced by rampant consumerism, an attitude that through hire purchase agreements people could realise their dreams and aspirations in an instant: of owning an electric cooker, a fridge or even a car. In 1957, the Prime Minister, Harold Macmillan, was able to say that most people had never had it so good. This was the world I was born into. My parents' new home of 1959, which I describe in detail as I remember it, was typical of the time. Yet the Second World War still hung heavily over our lives into the 1960s. Neighbours, parents of school friends and school teachers had served in the armed forces between 1939 and 1945, although to me as a child the war seemed a long way off. Such is the perception of time for the young when a year can seem like an epoch and the previous decade the far and distant past.

The first event that I can recall from the wider world was the wedding of Princess Margaret to Anthony Armstrong-Jones in 1960. This also happened to be the first year that I knew by date, and until I started writing I had not appreciated that this wedding was the first national event I was aware of, but so it was. Reading a draft of part of the book, a friend said to me: you mention the Cold War, but you don't mention the Cuban Missile Crisis. Well that is quite simply because I remember the Cold War; it was part of the framework or background to everyday life in my first decade, but I don't remember that particular crisis. I heard the name Khrushchev on the radio a lot around this time but I'm sure that the first time I heard of President Kennedy was the day he was assassinated. The book is selective. As I wrote, many of my childhood memories, including personal adventures or misadventures and recollections of current affairs, fell to the 'cutting room floor'. I do not attempt to comment on every news story or television programme I remember. So, recollections of the Vietnam War, the unfolding crisis in Biafra and at home, the conviction of the Kray Brothers and the Moors Murderers do not fit my narrative, even though I can recall all these news stories, mostly courtesy of the early evening BBC television news. There are also many TV programmes that I liked and remember, such as *Dr Finlay's Casebook*, *Z Cars* and *The Man From U.N.C.L.E.*, which are not featured in my story. To have included everything would have resulted in a long and unreadable mush of memories and no clear story. I talk of things that made a big impression on me, like the first time I saw *Doctor Who*, heard a Beatles song or watched the Apollo space missions on TV. It is a random list, but it is authentic.

The 1960s was a fast-moving decade. It has been described as a period of tumultuous change and the most transformative decade of modern times. Certainly, for me as a young teenager in 1969, the year 1960 seemed like a distant past. This may be in part the perspective of childhood when time passes more slowly, but the pace of change in many spheres of life was quite striking. Whilst some look back with affection to the period − it was retrospectively named the 'Swinging Sixties' − and talk of the sense of optimism they felt at the time, I found some of the progress painful and mourned the passing of certain things. I reacted against the modern suburbia I was brought up in. In many ways I should be grateful for growing up in a clean, comfortable and safe environment, but I couldn't help finding it boring and unconsciously I was searching for a more interesting world: the countryside, Victorian Birkenhead, and finally as a child I found a world I loved on holiday in Ireland. But the last holiday there in 1969 when I was 14 unexpectedly brought my childhood to a close.

My instinct when young was to explore the past through reading, drawing − even a bit of fieldwork − but also by talking to older people I encountered, many of whom had been born before 1900; so, as I wrote, a sub-theme of the book emerged of how in the 1960s, Victorian ways of life and Victorian objects remained a part of everyday life in opposition sometimes to the bright, new, shiny 1960s. But it was slipping away rapidly, and we just caught the tail end of the Victorian world before it was largely snuffed out by the inexorable march of progress. I bring to these pages some of the people I met − some of them Victorian, some nameless, but snapshots of people I encountered who, in one way or another represented a way of life that was rapidly disappearing: people like Harry Henshaw, Bert Richards (the Great Western Railway engine driver) and Catherine Connolly in Rock Ferry who lived over a quarter of her long life in Victorian England. I am fascinated by old things (academics talk of 'material culture') and heritage in situ, but I have increasingly come to value the role of ordinary people and their individual stories in making sense of the past and bringing it to life in a way that is colourful and intimate. These people would otherwise slip out of history but reference to their lives not only preserves a little of them but puts flesh on more academic histories and can also bring inanimate objects to life.

But this is chiefly my story of that decade: of one ordinary boy growing up in Merseyside suburbia in the 1960s. Perhaps it may fill a gap in the literature of the decade, recording some aspects, such as life at home, at school and on holiday, and offer a different perspective to conventional accounts of the time. This, I believe, is the chief purpose of this book.

Part One:

1955–59

1

Introductions

I have in front of me a copy of my certificate of birth. In black ink it states that I was born in Birkenhead on 20 June 1955. Of course, I know this. It was my mother who added that it was early on a Monday morning (about 5.30 a.m.) when I arrived in the world. The precise location was 'Annandale', a private nursing home in Storeton Road in Prenton, Wirral, Cheshire. Apparently, it was a sunny morning, windows were open and bees hummed around the cut flowers given to my mother. Storeton Road is not far from Higher Bebington, where my parents then lived. My father, Sydney Eveleigh, was from Yorkshire, and had served for several years as an engineer with the Blue Funnel Line. They had met two years earlier at the Tower Ballroom in New Brighton, and married in May 1954. I was the first born; two sisters were to follow.

The family home was '178', a 1930s semi on Higher Bebington Road that my mother's parents had purchased new in 1934. My mother, Barbara Wynne Jenkins, was the only daughter of Fred and Margaret Jenkins. Fred – and that *was* the sum total of his forename – was also a native of Birkenhead but had spent most of his early years in Liverpool. There he had trained as an architect at the Liverpool School of Architecture at the university. His wife, my maternal grandmother, was Margaret Coucil; she came from a respectable working-class family who lived in a council house in Knotty Ash, Liverpool. Fred and Margaret had married at St John's the Evangelist, Knotty Ash, in October 1928 and their daughter was born in Knotty Ash in August 1931. The jam butty mines of Knotty Ash, 'diddymen' and tickling sticks all lay in the future, but perhaps Fred and Margaret had ordered their coal from one 'Dodd, Coal Merchant', as the father of the entertainer Ken Dodd was a coal merchant in a big way in that part of Liverpool.

The decision to relocate across the Mersey to Wirral was not untypical at this time. With excellent links by ferry, underground electric trains and, after July 1934, by road through the Mersey Tunnel, Wirral was rapidly establishing itself as a popular dormitory area for working families in Liverpool. Facing Liverpool, the Wirral peninsula was predominantly industrial and urban in character – all the way from Birkenhead Docks for about 4 or 5 miles upriver to the entrance locks of the Manchester Ship Canal at Eastham. But away from the Mersey, it was a different world: a place of ridges and outcrops of sandstone, gorse and pine trees, patches of woodland and pretty winding roads linking its villages, hamlets and farmsteads. It contained some old sandstone churches with broach spires – which are easier to admire than explain – and also several windmills. The Wirral was ideal windmill country, windy and exposed, and in the 1930s a handful of these windmills still survived. Bidston Mill, which can be seen from Liverpool, was the first windmill to be preserved in Britain, in 1894. The head of Wirral faces out to Liverpool Bay. Here is true coastline containing several small seaside towns like New Brighton, Hoylake and West Kirby, which expanded after the opening of the Wirral Railway in the late nineteenth century.

Bidston Mill, a typical Wirral tower windmill. It dates from the early 1800s and consists of a three-storey brick tower. It worked until 1875, replacing an earlier timber post mill destroyed by fire in 1791. From a postcard used in 1924.

Cumbrous round arched doorways, pebbledash and stained glass in the windows: typical 1930s semis in Larchwood Drive off Town Lane, Higher Bebington.

So, Wirral was ripe for development and this was no isolated phenomenon. From the late 1920s and through the '30s, the development of new suburban estates, typically on the edges of towns and cities, was rapidly accelerating. The building of local authority estates had begun shortly after the end of the First World War to ease a chronic national housing shortage but by 1939 they had been outnumbered roughly two to one by privately built houses aimed at a new class of property owners. It was in these inter-war years that Middlesex, for example, largely succumbed to concrete, bricks and Portland cement (except for some generous grass verges and golf courses) and when several parts of Wirral acquired a distinctly suburban character.

Wirral suburbia was no different from suburbia anywhere. Indeed, one particular feature of 1930s housing is that it really did not matter where you were: it all looked pretty much the same – from Sidcup in Kent, most of Middlesex, Westbury on Trym in Bristol to extensive developments in Birmingham and Liverpool – and elsewhere. Whilst there were a few detached houses, and bungalows were quite popular, the greater part of this new wave of housing consisted of the three-bed semi, typically rendered in grey or brown pebbledash with cumbrous round arch open porches over and around the front door. They were laid out in avenues, ways and lanes, and the odd boulevard, but never or rarely was the name 'street' applied. Whilst ribbon development out of town of semis on busy roads was common, the typical development followed the garden suburb ideal that had emerged in the 1890s. The idea of a street conjured up a way of life that was the antithesis of the new estates, a world of dense town housing, some of it with backyard WCs, trams rattling by, smoky brick and little greenery. Life in the 1930s brought the opportunity for some of 'living the dream', of acquiring a home in a spaciously laid-out suburb with open country most likely nearby, but with the assurance that the new home had gas (for cooking), electricity (for lighting, the wireless set and the laundry iron), good drains, a bathroom and an indoor WC.

Such was 178 Higher Bebington Road, and when my maternal grandparents moved in there with their little infant daughter in February 1934, they

Christ Church, Kings Road, Higher Bebington. Designed by Walter Scott (1811-75) it was consecrated on 24 December 1859. The tower and spire were added in 1885. The Vicarage – also built of Storeton stone – is on the left.

were very likely home owners for the very first time. And 178 was close to open countryside. Higher Bebington Road was a 1930s development that ran downhill through former heathland towards Lower Bebington. The two settlements of Lower and Higher Bebington are about a mile apart and connected by a main road that runs all the way from New Ferry to Birkenhead, changing name several times on its route, although on its passage through Higher Bebington we simply referred to it as the 'Main Road'.

Lower Bebington was – and remains – the more important of the two, with an attractive parish church, St Andrew's – a sandstone church and one of those Wirral churches with a broach spire – municipal offices in Mayor Hall, and a railway station on the main line between Birkenhead and Chester. Between the railway and the banks of the Mersey lie New Ferry and Port Sunlight. Brunel's famous steam ship, the *Great Eastern*, was broken up on the beach at New Ferry in 1889–90 and it is claimed that it is still possible to find slivers of wrought iron from the hull in the sands of the beach. Port Sunlight, a model industrial village, was begun in 1889 by William Hesketh Lever (1851–1925) to provide homes for the workforce of his famous soap works. With its pretty cottages recalling vernacular building traditions, formal gardens and imposing art gallery, Port Sunlight is like nothing else on Wirral – except perhaps for Thornton Hough, a rural estate village of similar architecture that Lever also laid out.

Higher Bebington lies about a mile or so up this main road past the new grammar school, which had opened in September 1931 in what was then virtually open countryside. It was a village of small farms, quarries and stone cottages chiefly occupied by quarry workers and farm labourers. There was also a scattering of large red brick houses standing in their own grounds and typically screened from the road by tall trees: these were usually occupied by wealthy merchants and professional people who worked in Liverpool. On Kings Road, part of the main road heading towards Birkenhead, a parish church had been added in the late 1850s and, like so many Victorian churches and church restorations of the time, was finished in a textbook version of thirteenth-century ecclesiastical architecture. It was built of the hard, creamy white Storeton sandstone that had been quarried in the village since Roman times. Close up, chisel marks on the blocks used for the walls and buttresses can be clearly seen. They give the exterior walls a robust finish – like the 'rusticated' stonework of classical architecture – contrasting with the smoothly finished stonework around the windows and doors: these chisel

Higher Bebington windmill and outbuildings in the 1960s.

marks stand as a silent and unwritten memorial to the forgotten local men who hewed each building block out of the quarried stone ...

The centre of Higher Bebington was Village Road, which climbed from the main road (Teehey Lane) towards the wooded Storeton Ridge. Village Road contained a rather handsome Arts and Crafts style village hall – the Victoria Hall of 1897 – a straggle of stone cottages, some Victorian red brick shops and houses, three public houses (the Royal Oak, which carried a date stone of 1739, and then further up the hill, the George Hotel and the Traveller's Rest). Near the top end of the village, at the end of Mill Brow, there was an early nineteenth-century windmill and just beyond the mill, a large and deep quarry that remained a going concern until the late 1950s. The windmill had ceased working around 1901 and by 1934 it presented a forlorn spectacle: its sails and external timber gallery had been removed and its cap had blown off in a storm the previous year, but the red brick tower, still and silent, remained a familiar landmark visible on the approach to the village, especially from Lower Bebington, and provided a focal point and some character to this otherwise unremarkable village.

The top end of Village Road ended at a crossroads where it met Mount Road. The Traveller's Rest stood on one corner and opposite was a small corner shop. Across the road were Storeton Woods, which contained several disused quarries of the same Storeton sandstone hidden amongst the scots pine, birch and oak. Mount Road followed the ridge and in the Birkenhead direction crossed into Prenton, where it became Storeton Road. And that takes us back to my first few days in Annandale nursing home ...

2

Inside 178

A terse entry in my grandfather's diary for Saturday, 2 July 1955, records, 'Barbara came home from Annandale. Meaney used his car.' Edward (Ted) Meaney lived next door with his wife, Gwen. Fred had also recorded the delivery of a pram and cot in readiness on the two previous days. Margaret, my grandmother, was no longer there. She had died suddenly of a stroke in September 1953. For Monday, 18 July, my grandfather wrote 'Baby 4 weeks old today'. But he had not long to live. Fred had terminal cancer and made his last diary entry on 30 August. He died just a few days later.

We were to leave 178 just before my fourth birthday in 1959. I was happy there. I recall a tranquil and comfortable home and when it came to leave, I experienced nostalgic regret and sadness for the first time. The houses in Higher Bebington Road were built by Ben Davies, who was responsible for several other developments in the area. The interior that I distantly recall was fitted out and furnished largely as my grandparents had arranged it in the 1930s and '40s.

Oak panelling in the hall and stained glass at the front were standard but my architect grandfather specified that these were omitted. Of the houses built by Davies in Higher Bebington Road, only 178 lacked these features, which Fred doubtless regarded as pastiche. The interior décor was different from the neighbouring houses, with furnishings, pictures and ornaments that reflected my grandfather's interest in art and his circle of artist and craftsmen friends in Liverpool.

Fred was a member of the Sandon Studios Society, a club of architects, artists and sculptors, founded in 1905, that met in the Bluecoat Chambers, an early Georgian building in the centre of the city. One of his close friends was the well-known Liverpool sculptor, Herbert Tyson Smith (1883–1972): Fred

Fred Jenkins (centre) with Harold Hinchcliffe Davies, a well-known Liverpool architect, and his wife Nora, photographed by Edward Chambré Hardman at a café in Avignon between 10-13 June 1926.

owned several pieces by Herbert, including a beautiful small green bronze figure of a woman. Another of his friends was the photographer Edward Chambré Hardman (1898–1988), whose house and studio in Rodney Street is now owned by the National Trust. Hanging on the wall were original drawings and paintings by artists he knew, including an oil on canvas portrait of Margaret painted by another Sandon Studios member, the painter Henry Carr (*c.* 1872–1937). There were Japanese prints – a fine engraving of an early-Victorian steam ship, the *Archimedes*, which I remember was in the hall – and there was also a striking drawing of a nude by W.L. Stevenson, who went on to become the principal of the Liverpool School of Art; he was there when John Lennon was a (troublesome) student at the college in the late 1950s. As a young child I saw this drawing, which resembles the art of Eric Gill, as an indecipherable mass of scribbled lines.

The interior colours were muted. There was a lot of cream and green and the curtains in the front room consisted of floral prints. The dining room was papered in a light-cream textured wallpaper. The carpet was a mid-green, plain apart from a subtle twirl in the weave; the furniture included a mid-eighteenth-century panelled oak chest and a large, tall and dark oak bookcase – a wedding present to Fred and Margaret – which my mother later gave to the Salvation Army. There was also a large radio or wireless set – this was a Pye model, pre-war, with a cut out rising sun design over the speaker, a trademark design feature of the company. I also recall that there was an old-fashioned wind-up gramophone in the front room. Upstairs there was a separate bathroom and WC with a wooden seat, but the two rooms I remember most clearly are the morning room and the kitchen, doubtless because these were the rooms of everyday living. The morning room led off the hall and looked onto the side of the house and had an open tiled fireplace: the fire was lit regularly (with Co-op or Bryant & May's Pilot matches). The room was furnished with a pine kitchen table with a drawer at one end and three Windsor chairs. One of the few changes made by my parents in the home in the late 1950s was the addition of a television set, which was purchased around 1958. Whilst I have no recollection of the arrival of the TV, neither do I ever remember life without television, and this was to be another major influence on me – as it doubtless was for many children – through the following decade. The morning room led through into the kitchen, which occupied a single-storey extension at the rear of the house. This created a more spacious ground floor plan than some inter-war semis, which instead had a small 'kitchenette' squeezed into the basic rectangular house plan. Our kitchen was quarry tiled and fitted with a white fireclay sink and a scrubbed wooden drainboard. The back door led to the side of the house and another door opened into a small walk-in pantry cupboard.

The washing machine was a Hotpoint with a wringer that swung out over the drainboard on washing day. Cooking was done over a New World gas cooker. By 1939 roughly 90 per cent of British households cooked by gas and this was a very typical cooker of that period. It stood on short legs and was finished in a mottled grey and white enamel. As an infant, I had a near-fatal attraction to the row of brass keys that controlled the burners. These were just above the oven door and within easy reach of an infant. There was no safety 'push in and turn' device: turning the key simply opened the supply of the deadly town gas. And one morning, with my mother out of

Higher Bebington Road photographed probably shortly after completion in *c.* 1934; 178 was lower down on the left obscured in this view by the trees across the road.

A photograph of the dining room at 178 Higher Bebington Road looking towards the French windows, taken by Fred Jenkins in 1937.

the room, that is precisely what I did. Fortunately, my mother smelt the gas from upstairs and rushed down to find me 'grovelling' on the brown mat by the back door: this, I can remember. The doctor was called and, apparently, I was walked around the garden to clear my lungs.

The back kitchen door opened onto a concrete path that ran down the side of the house to the back garden: 178 was the left-hand house of the pair. There was a brick and concrete air raid shelter here that my grandfather had built in time for the Blitz. Of course, I knew nothing then of the Second World War and had no comprehension that the shelter was used by the family and some of the neighbours, including Gwen Meany – and her fur coat, apparently – in a time of great fear and stress during the height of the Blitz. Later, as an older child, I was told that my grandfather had a collection of firearms and, worried that in wartime they might have attracted the attention of the authorities, he buried them, wrapped in tarpaulin, in the concrete base of the shelter. I have often wondered if they were ever discovered …

Early memories are fragmentary and follow no chronology. I have a curious first-hand recollection of trying to steady myself by clutching the green stalks of plants in an attempt to stay upright but finding they were not strong enough to take my weight. The story I was later told was that on a fine spring day I had been put outside in my pram – a large black 'Silver Cross' vehicle – and had rocked it so vigorously that it upturned and I tumbled out, held precariously at about ground level by the pram straps. And so, was I found, dangling in a bed of bluebells, under an evergreen tree. I know this is a first-hand memory even though I must have been just ten months old. Another random memory is being taken to post a letter in Ted Meaney's car – the same one I was first brought home in. I clearly remember sitting in the front of the car for the short drive down the road and seeing the red post box ahead. When we stopped, I was lifted up to post the letter. Generally, there were few cars in the road. Most were black, and I remember the occasional passing of a rag and bone man with a horse and cart.

Without taking much notice, I was joined by a sister, Janet, who was born on 19 May 1957, also in Birkenhead. She was given Wynne as a middle name, a name shared by my mother and a great aunt, Lilias, one of Fred's sisters. It was a family name and a memory of Welsh ancestry. A pleasant recollection from about 1957 or 1958 is of sitting on the edge of the pram with Janet asleep under the covers as my mother took us with her, shopping in Lower Bebington. Then in the spring of 1959, I recall my first sequence of events. I was sent to stay with one of my mother's friends, a young woman called Ann Chadwick, at her family home, 57 Halkyn Street in Flint, a large late Victorian house with a long narrow garden near a brick-built chapel. Her father was one-time mayor of the town. Ann was unswervingly kind and lovely: she would shine a torch around the bedroom if I was frightened of the dark, provide me with limitless jugs of water so I could make any number of mud pies in her garden, and take me with her when she went shopping in Chester by train. Then one warm and sunny day when I was playing on my own in her garden, she suddenly announced it was time for me to return home. Ann used her brother's car – a black Vauxhall – to take me home and I sat in the front passenger seat as we drove to Bebington in fine weather along country roads: I remember clearly the white iron fences bordering the fields, which are often seen in rural Cheshire. Immediately upon arriving home, I was led upstairs and holding my slightly grubby hands tight at my side, there I saw – fast asleep – a new sister, in my bed! Helen had been born at home a few days earlier on 11 May.

I also knew we were to leave 178 and preparations must have been at an advanced state by then, for on 13 June 1959 we relocated to a brand-new detached house about half a mile further up the hill in Higher Bebington. But I was not present to witness this momentous event. Doubtless to lessen my parents' lot, I was packed off to stay for a few days, while the move took place, with an older couple my mother knew – the Websters, who lived in Lower Bebington. I did not particularly enjoy this second short stay. I vividly remember on a fine day, walking around the circular ornamental path in their back garden singing a tuneless song about making my way home. The Websters were sitting in the sun and peevishly asked me if I wanted to go home. I was taken aback and made my apologies. I had not intended to cause offence and denied I wanted to leave, when this was almost certainly the case.

Opposite: Detail of a 25 inch to the mile Ordnance Survey Map of Higher Bebington, 1874. North is top. Orchard Way later occupied most of field 78. The sycamore trees behind Elm House are marked. Well Lane is bounded by Claremont and Elm House. The windmill is seen centre. Storeton Woods are just visible left of Mount Road whilst the Higher Bebington Freestone Quarries are near the National School. The Storeton Tramway passes under Mount Road. Mill Road School was later built on the allotment gardens, replacing the National School.

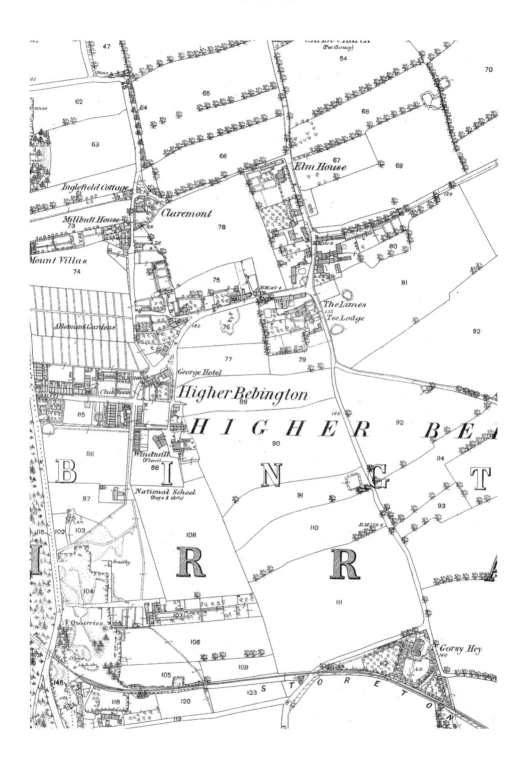

3

Suburban Spread

So when I left the Websters, it was for a new home, 1 Orchard Way. The contrast with 178 could not have been greater. This was the last house to be completed in a new road – a cul de sac – of twenty-nine new homes that consisted entirely of bungalows apart from three detached houses that stood together – numbers one, three and five – on the left-hand side near its junction with Well Lane. The builder was a man called Bradshaw and he must have begun the road about 1957.

As the first house on the left, our new home occupied the corner plot and had gardens front, side and back. The side garden bounded Well Lane, which in 1959 was a narrow, leafy lane of tall trees with a pair of large, late Victorian red brick houses across the road, 'Cabra' and 'Craigside'. Further up and across the road from our new home there was a derelict nursery in an old shallow quarry where the bright yellow sandstone – which was never far below the surface in our garden – had once been extracted. The nursery contained three old glass houses in front of an old and high wall of crumbling brick. Above Orchard Way, for Well Lane climbs from the main road up to Mill Road, the road narrowed slightly and was lined with craggy outcrops of soft yellow sandstone. And more trees.

At the back, our garden looked over and down on the large well-kept garden of Elm House, a large old house occupied by an accountant, Charles F. Stead, which fronted the main road (Kings Road at this point). The house, I clearly remember, had chimney stacks at each gable end and another in the middle, and the garden was laid out with lots of small neat beds and narrow paths. To the right of Elm House, our back garden looked onto a large area of rough grass containing an old tree that extended downhill towards the main road, and this was very probably once part of the garden of Kings Farm, which had been demolished before the war.

My parents loved their new home and were proud of it, especially as it was a detached house, modern and new; but for me, Orchard Way cut a gash of concrete, rough-cast rendering and harsh, pinky-red fletton brick through this semi-rural netherland. The new road was made up with low walls and gate posts of flettons to each dwelling; gates were mostly of ornate, scrolled mild steel; the pavements were made of dimpled concrete slabs and even the street lamps were of pre-cast concrete, probably by Revo of Tipton in the Black Country.

Elm House was soon to go. Within about a year of our arrival it was demolished to make way for a new development: the Elm House Estate, which consisted of five semi-detached houses. Another development nearby of the late 1950s completed before we moved in was Bentfield Gardens; this took over the site of a large house and garden, Bentfield House, which was demolished to make way for the new homes. So, Orchard Way was not one isolated building venture but part of a second, post-war wave of suburbanisation that was to further change the face of Higher Bebington. For several years after we moved in, the sound of building construction was never far away.

Architecturally, the new homes of the late 1950s and '60s marked a clear break with the first phase of suburban development of the 1930s. Gone were the round arched porchways, bay windows with twinkling stained glass and the Tudor-inspired half-timbered gables. And instead of pebbledash, the new homes were more usually finished in rough-cast, fletton brick and white weatherboarding. But the deployment of these features made little or no reference to the past. The new houses were all about the 'here and now' of 1960s living: Tudor was definitely out; contemporary was in.

The dominant and unifying feature was the large timber-framed picture window. These were rarely in bays but set flush with the line of the wall. Typically, there was one or sometimes two large fixed panes of glass with a small upper transom window that opened for ventilation. But it was all about light. The interior of 1 Orchard Way was very light, thanks to five large windows in the rear elevation, a front door of hammered glass accompanied by a low wide window over the stairs. The living room, or lounge, had large windows front and back plus a single French window opening onto the back garden. Many of the houses of this period were box-like, built to a simple rectangular plan, but Bradshaw's three houses in Orchard Way had an interesting staggered front. The garage, with a prominent gable and double pitched roof, projected forwards towards the front gate, then set back in the centre was the front door and stair window – the roof swept down at this point – and further back again was a full-height wall, with windows to the living room window and bathroom above.

The walls were rendered in rough-cast cement, except for the centre portion of the front elevation containing the glass front door, which was left as brick. The end gable of the house was relieved by an external chimney stack that ran the full height of the wall and gable to the stack on the roof. This was also left in brick, doubtless to make a feature of it. The chimney flue served the open fireplace in the living room, which contained an open fire grate and a back boiler providing hot water to radiators on the ground floor and a chrome-plated towel rail in the bathroom. There was no heating in the bedrooms, and the bathroom – heated by just the towel rail – was inclined to be a little chilly in winter. The open fireplace was a simple tiled design with a matching tiled hearth. Smokeless fuel was burned – Sunbright Number 2 – and this was stored in a square concrete coal bunker on the corner of the concrete path at the back of the house. There was a lot of concrete in Orchard Way.

Exterior paintwork on the 1930s semis was inclined to be dark and sombre – black, navy or royal blue, green or cream dominated – and casements were often painted cream to contrast with the frame, painted a darker colour. But from the late 1950s there was an explosion of bright new colours on the new houses. My parents chose a pale sky blue for the exterior paintwork of our new house, whilst the rough cast was initially painted a pale yellow, although this was soon replaced by brilliant white in Snowcem masonry paint. Other colours on neighbouring houses included light turquoise green, primrose yellow and mauve; white became popular, too. Our pale blue was also a very popular choice in the early 1960s: our plastic toilet seat was pale blue, our washing up bowls were usually pale blue, and around 1963 or 1964 it was also a fashionable colour for motor cars: some of the first Ford Cortinas and Triumph Heralds, I recall, were available in a two-tone scheme of pale blue and white.

As a boy of 4, once Elm House had been demolished and the roofs put on the new houses at the bottom of our garden, I was amazed to see they had no chimney stacks. This was another remarkable break with the past. For three or four centuries, virtually all houses in Britain had been built with chimneys; now they had gone. Instead of an open fire, these houses were fitted with oil fired central heating. Each house had an open-sided 'car port' at the side for the family car (few households owned more than one car in the 1960s) and behind this was a large steel oil tank.

The building continued all around us. On the corner of Town Lane and the main road, the Co-op built a supermarket – a modern flat-roofed building of pale brown brick – which opened about 1960. I remember being struck by the vastness of the interior, which set it apart from the other shops I knew in the village. It was bright and uncluttered and there were electric wall heaters glowing orange high up on the walls: I thought these were particularly futuristic. Then there was the novelty of making our own choices of groceries and other things stacked on the long straight shelves, putting them in a wire basket and paying at the tills near the large glass entrance – the term 'checkout' was not current then. At the tills my mother was always asked for her Co-op dividend number, which was 61916, a nice symmetrical and easy to remember number. Soon after the Co-op opened this bright new and shiny supermarket, the old grocery store nearby run by Griffiths selling the traditional grocery lines of ham, butter, cheese and tea, closed.

Around the same time, the old Royal Oak closed to be replaced by a new pub nearby, the Acorn (what else of course!). This detached building sat in a large tarmac car park behind a low wall, not of the local sandstone but rather incongruously of slabs of Welsh slate. Next to the pub on a piece of wasteland, a petrol station was completed in March 1964. Selling Fina petrol, it was opened by Ken Dodd. I was incredibly excited and impressed that a TV personality (the term 'celeb' had not been coined then) as famous as Ken Dodd was coming to Higher Bebington. Alas, I did not manage to see him.

The derelict nursery across the road from 1 Orchard Way on Well Lane was also developed about the same time and the by then heavily vandalised greenhouses were replaced by five or six houses with white weatherboarding and the usual large picture windows. It was also around this time that the upper section of Well Lane, above Orchard Way, was widened and the rough sandstone outcrops became less prominent.

Very close to the top of Well Lane on Mill Road there was further road widening, which resulted in the shortening by about 10ft of a lovely old stone cottage that bore a date stone for 1720. We called this Henshaw's Cottage after the owner/occupier, although it was more properly known as Inglefield Cottage. In the early 1960s, it was the home of Harold (Harry) Henshaw and his wife. My father had befriended Harry in the George Hotel and one day when my father and I were passing by we were invited in to look at their garden. I recall that Harry and his wife were a friendly old couple and in front of their house was a picturesque old-fashioned cottage garden; this had an arched opening in a tall privet hedge that led from the front flower garden into a vegetable plot at the back where there was a standpipe with an old tap. The problem was that this long low dwelling was situated at right angles to the road – and it stuck out – creating a bottleneck and doubtless an accident black spot for speeding motorists. So, the cottage had to be shortened. The end gable was rebuilt, bringing it into line with the rest of the road, but the old front wall of mellowed sandstone was replaced by one made of concrete blocks.

There was no end to the building. Every spare patch of land was built on until the old village was caught in a pincer movement, one that had, of course, begun in the 1930s, but which was largely complete by the end of the '60s. A row of shops had been built on the main road (Teehey Lane) before the war, but if our shopping took us to the shops in Village Road, then we talked of 'going to the village' as if it were a different place with its own distinctive personality. The new houses were typically occupied by school teachers, civil servants and policemen, and they gave their houses novelty names like 'Amron' (that was Norma spelt backwards) and 'Pequeño' – that was the Smalls, who came to live in one of the new houses where the nursery had once stood. But the villagers, living in Victorian terraces and little stone cottages, were for me, as a child, virtually a race apart: some of the village children I met at school seemed just that little bit poorer and scruffier.

The Royal Oak was modernised and became the offices of an architectural practice. Next to it was a sooty dark brick terrace of thirteen small houses with long gardens at the front. This row was also placed at right angles to the road and, facing the river, was called Mersey Terrace. It was built about 1882 and on several occasions when I was about 9 or 10, I remember seeing a very old woman by the houses who could have passed for an original resident. Her white hair was tied back in a bun and she wore a long black dress that would not have looked out of place sixty or seventy years earlier. At that age I took it for granted that all homes had bathrooms with shiny, heated towel rails, WCs with low level flushes and plastic toilet seats; but I suspect that – as in other villages and towns across Britain in the 1960s – some of the houses in Mersey View still lacked bathrooms and indoor WCs. The contrast with our own way of life, just about 400 yards away, could not have been greater.

So there were, for a while, two Higher Bebingtons: the old and the new, but it was the new suburbia that was coming to typify much of Wirral. A land of 'hatchbacks and pampas grass' was how one observer saw the Wirral later in the century. But the encroachment of suburbia was not confined to Wirral. Up and down the country, especially on the fringes of large towns and cities, villages and farmsteads were disappearing under a tide of new housing estates, both council built and private. Whilst this was progress, so far as improving the quality of the housing stock and therefore, standards of living for many people, it was almost invariably accompanied by the destruction of old buildings built according to local tradition and using local materials. The older structures blended with their surroundings. They enhanced the local landscape and confirmed a sense of place. Each building also carried stories and memories of local people, so their loss was accompanied by a diminution of local identity and character. Today we would describe this destruction as a loss of 'heritage in situ' – it still goes on now, but in the 1960s it was happening on a devastating national scale.

4

Living in 1 Orchard Way

After the quiet tranquil life of 178, our new surroundings were chaotic and noisy. Noisy because for the first time there were other children around. I was later told that when I first saw them I just stared and stared in amazement, rather as the inhabitant of a New Guinea jungle might on his first encounter with a white missionary! There were (briefly) children across the road in the nearest Victorian house, 'Cabra', and then two boys in Number 3, the new house next door. Our new neighbours there were Peter and Daphne Savage from Caterham in Surrey and their two boys, Brian and John. Peter Savage was a civil servant and worked at Speke Airport, Liverpool, but we children always addressed them formally as Mr and Mrs Savage.

The chaos was probably simply the chaos that comes with any house move. I remember an untidy kitchen with things piled high in front of the serving hatch and of playing with a blue and yellow plastic submarine – a present on my fourth birthday, which occurred just a few days after the move. The chaos extended across much of the garden, as Bradshaw's men had used this last plot as an ad hoc builders' yard and dumping ground. There was sand and cement everywhere, leftover bricks, broken asbestos board and a barrel on its side leaking tar.

We quickly settled in, however. My father cleared the rubbish, and used the loose bricks to build a low retaining wall in front of the raised bank at the rear of the back garden. The large sycamore tree in the corner of the garden, overlooking Well Lane, was cut down, although strangely, a tall stump remained for the rest of our time there. Grass seed was spread front and back to create lawns and my father purchased a large number of hybrid tea roses: names I recall are 'Peace', a creamy white rose, pink 'Margaret' and 'Cleopatra', which had bright yellow and pink flowers. A beech hedge was planted behind the low front wall that extended from the gate to Well Lane, and then eventually a woven timber fence erected along the Well Lane side of the house.

Peter and Daphne Savage also had their sycamore tree felled early on, but our other tree remained, along with a tall and dense hawthorn tree to its right; they were to be a source of some rancour with our new neighbours across the rear fence when the new houses were built. But I loved our sycamore tree. It was taller than the house and, looking up through it branches, I used to imagine how it had once looked out over a very different landscape of orchards and nurseries, large gardens and old houses and open heathland and gorse stretching downhill towards Lower Bebington. Intriguingly, a 25in-to-the mile Ordnance Survey map of the 'Township of Higher Bebington', surveyed in 1874, seems to show this tree along with three others in their actual positions on the rear border of Elm House. Sycamore trees are noted for their longevity and ours was an old specimen: the grey bark of the lower trunk was flaky – a sign of a mature tree – and could be peeled off in patches. I guess the tree might have dated, therefore, from the second half of the eighteenth century.

Within the house, my mother established a contemporary 1960s interior. The house had a very different feel to 178. Lighter, more open – and modern – but perhaps a little less cosy. I noticed that the light switches and sockets throughout the house were different: the switches and sockets in 178 were of dark brown Bakelite, now they were white plastic and almost flush with the wall. The old two-pin plugs of Bakelite of Mum's iron and other appliances had to be changed to the new type with three squarish pins that we use today. The hall was floored in cedar strip, whilst a plain turquoise green carpet was chosen for the stairs and gallery landing. The walls throughout the hall and landing were a light peach colour. Joinery was brilliant white. As most friends and neighbours had patterned carpets in their hallways, I thought this plain carpet struck a particularly modern and sophisticated note. Eventually a feature wall in the hall was created by papering it with Vymura wallpaper in a rich, dark design of something like peacock feathers. My parents' bedroom was also startlingly modern and different. The walls were painted in mauve matt emulsion; the carpet was purple with a whitish fleck. They also bought a new modern bedroom suite in teak shortly after we moved in with a low dressing table, matching chest of drawers and headboard (with integrated side cupboards) for their bed.

In the living room or 'lounge', the television was placed in the corner to the right of the fireplace and in the other corner by the window there was a bright red and cream Dansette record player, which stood on thin black tapering legs. A two-seat sofa – we called it a settee – which came from 178 was placed against the back wall; there were two G-Plan armchairs with wooden armrests and yellow and black striped upholstery, and not long after we moved in my parents bought a low 'television' chair in a burnt orange colour. This chair was very low and comfortable, but lacked arms as the idea was that two or more chairs could be placed together to create a flexible seating arrangement in front of the television. Two wall lamps were added to the back wall and they provided a softer, cosier atmosphere than the 'big light' in the ceiling. Around 1963, a contemporary-style teak bureau, with lower sliding doors and short, splayed tapering legs, was added to the back wall near the door into the hall. For many years this had a most wonderful strong scented smell of teak oil whenever it was opened. There were very few ornaments or pictures: it was all very uncluttered and minimalist.

In front of the fireplace there was a thick-pile woollen rug in navy, turquoise and emerald green. The original fireplace and hearth consisted of beige-coloured tiles but later in the 1960s it was replaced by a Parkray stove set in a new surround made of small blocks of light grey limestone. These stone fire surrounds became popular in the late '60s and were usually known as 'Cotswold stone' fireplaces. As a boy, I thought this replacement was fabulous! I loved the little inset shelf, just the right size for one small ornament. The shallow mantelshelf running across the top of the fireplace was left largely bare, but one of the few ornaments was a glass-bottomed pewter tankard that had been presented to my dad when he left Birkenhead Technical College (he taught motor mechanics there for a few years). The fire was lit daily in cold weather, often with an electric poker, a device resembling a giant hair dryer or paint gun that was stuck into the fuel and made a horrible rattle. It was not always effective.

The kitchen was at the rear of the house and flanked by the living room and dining room; it was linked to the latter by a service hatch of sliding, spotted glass. It faced the back garden and my father had a glazed stable door fitted so we could enjoy fresh air in mild weather. Although it was not large, this room was quickly established as the main family living space where my mother cooked and washed and where we ate our meals. My toys were stored in a box in the corner and here we would sometimes play and get ready for

1 Orchard Way, Higher Bebington, built 1959 seen in c 1961 with the sycamore tree behind the house and Barbara Eveleigh, David's mother – waving at the camera – holding his youngest sister, Helen; the lounge with the bathroom above are on the left.

The Tricity Viscount electric cooker from The Ironmonger, 23 March 1957; the same model was purchased for 1 Orchard Way in 1959.

school, and after the evening meal I often sat at the kitchen table, drawing, painting or doing my homework. The sink and drainboard were no longer separate items of fireclay and wood but an integrated fitting of stainless-steel set on fitted cupboards with flush doors. This represented the latest thinking. The fitted kitchen – promoting hygiene and convenience for the housewife – had emerged in the late 1930s but remained largely confined to theory, featured in architects' journals and lifestyle magazines, until after the war when house building resumed in the 1950s. A full-height pantry cupboard in the corner by the stable door connected to a Formica-covered worktop in front of the serving hatch to the dining room. In place of quarry tiles, the floor was finished in mid-blue vinyl tiles with a white marbling. They were made by Dunlop and went by the trade name of Semtex. The cupboard doors were painted pale blue; other joinery was white and the walls finished in a bright yellow, durable and washable wall paint with a slight sheen.

This kitchen was all-electric, with a Tricity Viscount cooker purchased new from the Co-op in Chester when we moved in: it cost £46 12s 6d. An electric kettle was bought with it. The cooker was cream. It had an oven, grill and two rings on the top with a rectangular hot plate for stewing; this latter device was always rather troublesome as it tended to corrode, shedding flakes of rust, to the consternation of my house-proud mother. The saucepans were aluminium, and stews such as Lancashire hot pot (which I never liked) were cooked in an oval, cream enamel stewing pot with a separate dimpled and domed lid. From our former home, my mother brought an old bread board of golden-coloured sycamore that she had for many years. The oldest item of kitchen equipment was a cream-painted set of scales – or more correctly, a weighing machine. I don't think this was ever used and it was stored at the back of the fitted cupboard below the sink; I was always fascinated by the apparent complexity of the mechanism. Our crockery was a mixed bag. There was some blue and white Cornish ware, some pale yellow and pale green plates and then a set of blue polka dot dinner and side plates by the well-known designer Susie Cooper (1902–95). This was a wedding present to my parents from my grandfather, Fred. I had an egg cup in the shape of a mauve elephant and later in the 1960s I acquired my first mug for drinking tea and coffee.

My grandparents' pine table survived the move to 1 Orchard Way, but not for long. On a summer's evening – probably in 1959 – when I was in bed, but awake, I remember hearing my parents 'walking' the pine table around to the garage at the front of the house. Its replacement was a modern little rectangular table with slightly curved sides, straight but slightly tapering legs of beechwood and a Formica top. And the colour? Pale blue. Although by and large I welcomed the contemporary, bright feel to our new home, and especially the kitchen, I always regretted the demotion to the garage of this characterful, old pine table with its scrubbed top, turned legs and drawer at one end. It did not survive the next move in 1970.

The space under the Formica worktop, which was opposite the cooker, was used to store the washing machine and to its right there was a meat safe. We didn't have a fridge – much to my mother's frustration – and instead made do with this old meat safe: a cream-painted cabinet with perforated panels of grey zinc and a single shelf that Fred had made before the war. Everything that might have been stored in a fridge – meat, butter, cheese and milk – was stored here. It may have kept the flies at bay but the temperature in the safe was little or no different from room temperature, and in warm weather keeping the milk fresh was a constant challenge. Sometime in the mid-1960s my mother acquired a thick white polystyrene milk cooler that could hold two-pint bottles. But the meat safe remained, an embarrassment to my mother and we three children for the eleven years we lived there; a day of two before we finally left the house, I broke it up and burned it, which I now think was a pity as it was quite a 'museum piece', as few survive.

The washing machine was the cream cabinet machine, a Hotpoint with a folding wringer, which had come with us from 178. Every Monday morning this was pulled out into the middle of the room next to the sink and then several loads of washing – all separated, of course, and ending with socks and underwear – were loaded one at a time into the machine's galvanised metal pot, which was filled with hot water. Soap powder such as Omo or Persil was added and then the washing was swirled round and round by the black plastic agitator, a paddle-like device driven by an electric motor in the bottom of the cabinet. Each load of washing was then passed through the electrically driven rubber wringer that swung out over the sink. The washing was manipulated by a pair of bleached wooden tongs. Once completed, the washing was pegged out on the washing line, which stretched across the lawn and was raised into the wind by a long wooden clothes prop. I can't recall how my mother dried clothes – what her 'plan B' was – when it rained.

The metal pot of this electric washing machine was a throwback to the traditional coal-fired wash copper – a cast-iron pot, usually – which was fixed in brickwork over a small grate in the scullery or wash house. Across Britain the lighting of the wash copper early on a Monday morning was once a routine weekly event and a lifetime sentence for women (although the lighting of the fire was often carried out by the man of the house). The washing was first soaked and stirred in the boiling or simmering water of the pot before being beaten or scrubbed in a galvanised iron dolly tub or kitchen sink. This older method of washing – sometimes updated with a gas boiler to supply the hot water – survived into the 1960s and even the '70s, and very likely was still carried on in some of the older houses in Bebington and Birkenhead at that time. So, electricity took away some of the hard graft, but my mother's wash day was still hard work. Mondays were a miserable day at home with restricted access to the kitchen until the end of the afternoon. This Hotpoint machine soldiered on until 1970, by which time I was nearly as embarrassed by it as the meat safe. Through the 1960s, many of our neighbours had graduated to twin tub machines in sparkling white: anything cream in the kitchen to me looked old-fashioned.

The serving hatch through to the dining room was little used as we rarely occupied this room. It was carpeted in a deep blue Kosset carpet (made in West Yorkshire) and became something of a mausoleum to 178, containing antique furniture and pictures that had belonged to my grandparents: the old oak chest, the top half of a Victorian mahogany bookcase displaying old books and china, and an eighteenth-century mahogany table together with a set of ladder-back and rush-seated chairs. Into this my mother introduced a table lamp using a Mateus rosé wine bottle as the lamp base; aged about 9 or 10, I thought this was the height of sophistication. Of course, although I then knew nothing about old bottles, I thought the oval-shaped green bottle looked 'old worlde', the sort of bottle that would have been familiar to an eighteenth-century ocean-going buccaneer. The room was little used. Occasionally my parents would serve dinner for guests there (usually after we had been packed off to bed) and it was used for dinner on Christmas Day and Boxing Day when we would eat off the Wedgwood porcelain dinner service – a design called Beaconsfield – which my parents had purchased shortly after we moved in.

Part 2:

1960–66

5

Starting School

Chronological time – as measured in the western Christian world – first entered my consciousness in 1960. At the time, my father banked with the Trustee Savings Bank in Birkenhead and when I was aged 4 or 5 he gave me a bronze medal issued by the bank; it was just a little larger and heavier than the pennies of the time. It carried the date, 1960. This was the first year I knew, and it was through this medal that I came to understand dates and time and became aware of the year we were living in. I then began to wonder when my parents had grown up; a distant era, I imagined – the 'olden days' – when lives were led in a dreamy sepia monochrome. I could never quite believe that life in the 1930s and '40s had been lived in the same strong colour as the world I inhabited.

Shiny, new pennies were minted each year from 1961 and we would always find one with the new date in our Christmas stocking, not much use – even then – as cash, but an effective marker of the passing of time. For Christmas 1963 I was given a red pocket diary for 1964 and that following year I made my own record, for the first time, of the events in my own rather limited world. Time then moved relatively slowly. By 1965 or 1966, the early '60s seemed some way off in the past and markers of time included the rate of new developments in Higher Bebington, other aspects of modernisation that I was aware of, like the decline of steam power on the railways and new models of cars, and even changes to the radio and television programmes. Another marker of time I became aware of around that time was a growing realisation that people who could be described as 'late middle-aged' – that is people in their 60s – had been born at the beginning of the century, about 1900. Old people, like my paternal grandmother, great aunts and anyone else I knew who was old, had been born before 1900 – that is, in the late 1800s. They, I came to understand, were Victorian.

Back to 1960: I began the year in a 'pre-school' state, which meant I was at home all day, learned little or nothing, roamed our new garden or played with my toys. A major part of the daily routine was following *Listen with Mother* on the radio and *Watch With Mother* on television, which consisted of a weekly cycle I remember clearly from Monday to Friday of *Picture Book, Andy Pandy, The Flower Pot Men, Rag Tag and Bobtale* and *The Wooden Tops*, in that order.

Incidentally, I saw each day of the week in my mind's eye in colour: for example, Tuesdays (*Andy Pandy* day) was pale green, Wednesdays, when the Flower Pot men garbled at each other with Weed, were a deep blue-grey, and Fridays, when I watched *The Wooden Tops*, were a watery dark red. This phenomenon is known as synesthesia, when one sensory or 'cognitive pathway' involuntarily triggers another. This short circuiting in my brain also extends to numbers, decades and months of the year. The colour palette is limited and the colours do not have the solidity and brightness of colours in a paint chart but are watery and fugitive. My 1950s are coloured a light, creamy yellow, whilst I see the '60s as mid-grey, and the '70s were to be a sombre dark green ...

For much of the day there was no broadcasting of programmes, and up to just before 5 p.m. the television screen was filled with the dull, dreary test card that featured a complicated design of rectangles, squares and concentric circles in black, white and grey. Television in the 1960s was resolutely black and white – or rather, many shades of grey. The test card gave way to daytime programming every Saturday when *Grandstand* started around lunchtime. Daytime television was also broadcast on bank holidays and it also made a one-off appearance on Friday, 6 May 1960 when the wedding of Princess Margaret to Anthony Armstrong-Jones was broadcast live from Westminster Abbey by the BBC. It was watched by 20 million viewers, and that included my mother and me (my sisters would have been too young). I did not have any particular interest in the wedding – that the royal wedding dress was designed by Norman Hartnell will have completely passed me by – but this was almost certainly the first event from the wider world that touched my life, and anything was better than the test card.

I must have started school within a week or so of the Royal wedding. So, Rag Tag and Bob Tail and all the rest became a little part of my past as daily life for the first time involved a regime of getting up to go to school. The bright blue railings that fronted Town Lane Infants School were just a

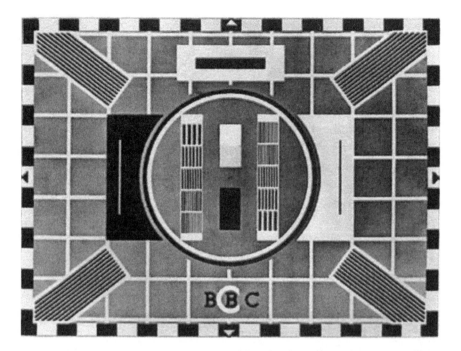

The BBC test card of the early 1960s. Occasionally the television set broke down and when this happened it was repaired by Strothers of Birkenhead who used to take it away in their van.

few minutes' walk from 1 Orchard Way downhill in the direction of Lower Bebington. The school was established in the immediate post-war period and was typical of infant schools built across Britain in the late 1940s and early '50s. The interior design and layout marked a major break with traditional school architecture and design. As a Bristol newspaper of 1956 wrote of these new infant schools, 'all of them are a small world of plastic, plate glass and pastel shades'. In place of regimented lines of desks, the light and airy classrooms were set out with an informal arrangement of low tables and child-size plywood chairs, doubtless to promote the idea of a safe and informal learning environment.

I have two memories of my first day at school. At lunchtime, or 'dinner hour', I went to the canteen for the school dinner, found myself a place on a bench at a long table to eat and was abruptly pushed off backwards, head over heels, by a boy with curly blond hair called Stephen Cassia. He claimed I was sitting in his place. I was not prepared for such aggression – nor, over the ensuing weeks – for being punched by some of the rougher boys in the stomach and winded. I had to learn to make a fist to defend myself but I was not a natural fighter or ruffian. My other recollection from that first morning at school is of being asked by a smiling Mrs Luck, our teacher, to fetch some crayons: crayons … what was a crayon? A type of crane? I had no idea and looked around in confusion and in vain for a toy crane. But the school issue crayons – thick, waxy sticks (smelling of stearine) in bright primary colours used for drawing and colouring in – soon became a daily part of school life, along with powder paints, sums and the morning register.

In my second year at school, our class teacher was Miss Fairhurst. Every morning she would read out the names of the forty or so children in the class in alphabetical order and tick them off in her register. One morning – early in the school year – when she reached my name, I replied 'Yes Miss Hair-first.' There was a ripple of laughter from some of the other children. This was very probably my first joke. And it was quite unintentional – well, at first. However, I came to repeat my spoonerism most mornings, sensing the anticipation, knowing I would receive a smile from the teacher and trigger a ripple of laughter from the rest of the class. Then we used to settle down on our little chairs at our little tables for our morning lessons in arithmetic and learning to write; there were also easier activities such as colouring in squared paper with the wax crayons and painting. Good work received a tick from our teacher and the best was rewarded with a little adhesive gold star stuck on the top. Then in descending order there were silver stars followed by red, blue and green; the lowest reward was a yellow star. I used to like getting a star …

Mid-morning was playtime and, unless the weather was very wet, we were let outside to play on the school playground. It was at this point in the day that we were given our free school milk. We each collected our small bottle of milk, a third of a pint, from milk crates left in the school yard. These bottles were an exact miniature version of the pint glass bottles in which milk was delivered to most homes in the 1960s: they even had the same silver tin foil tops. The provision of free school milk was established by Clement Atlee's Labour Government in 1945 when the Free School Milk Act was passed, giving every school child under the age of 18 the right to a third of a pint of milk each day to promote better nutrition. This might have been a laudable aim, but in warm weather, left in the sun, the milk often turned sour and the cream at the top curdled. Then in wintry weather the opposite occurred. In the bitterly cold and long winter of 1962–63, when the school playground became a treacherous ice rink – or a series of 'slides' in the ice made by the children – the milk froze, pushing the silver foil tops off the neck of the bottle. I quickly decided to forgo the free milk for the rest of my school career and hardly noticed later in the decade when Harold Wilson's government cut free milk to all secondary schools.

Another enduring memory of those first days at school is standing in the school hall for morning assembly. As an infant this space seemed huge. It had a polished wood block flooring and a piano. We learned the Lord's Prayer, which we chanted, standing, with our heads bowed and our eyes shut tight. I did not understand the words – other than that it was about someone named Harold, the daily bread delivery and not trespassing in next door's garden. But the words and cadence of this prayer were somehow comforting. A pleasant memory too, is of assembly on a fine day, probably in spring: sunshine flooded in through the large windows of the hall, occasionally interrupted by passing white clouds, as we sang *All Things Bright and Beautiful*. From first hearing I liked this uncomplicated and optimistic Victorian hymn and ever since, the words and melody have been indelibly linked in my mind with sunshine, pale yellow walls and parquet flooring.

In the autumn of 1962, I started at Mill Road Junior School, just a short walk from home up Well Lane and then left along Mill Road at Henshaw's Cottage in the direction of the old windmill. The school badge depicted the windmill in yellow on black and was built in 1914. Built of brick with some stone detailing, it was a very typical building of its type from the early 1900s. The classroom windows were large, with multiple panes and transoms opened by long window poles with brass hooks. The windows were placed high in the wall, doubtless to shut out the distractions of the outside world to the children within. Inside, the lower part of the classroom walls were lined in glossy, dark green or brown tiles. There were four classrooms at the rear of the plan, which were used for the older children aged 9 to 11. They were accessed by a wide draughty corridor and looked out onto the school sports field, which extended as far as Mount Road and in view of the slightly forbidding dark green pine trees of Storeton Woods. There was a large assembly hall that was used for exams and assemblies where we learned to sing *Rule Britannia*, *Land of Hope and Glory* and *Jerusalem*. Each classroom had an open fireplace but the school was centrally heated by a coal fired boiler. There was always a large pile of coal for the boiler around the back of the building, and responsibility for this lay with Mr Yates, the school caretaker, a tall, lanky older man with a drooping moustache and a flat cap. Compared to Town Lane Infants School, Mill Road School seemed rather dark, gloomy and daunting.

Flanking the outer edge of the two yards were toilet blocks for the children. On the boys' side, one of the child-size WCs contained a perfectly shaped, solid and immoveable turd. Incredibly, it remained there for the entire four years I was at the school and had turned a mossy green. I was amazed that no one apparently made any attempt to remove it. I pulled the chain several times to flush it away, but it remained stuck fast to the bottom of the toilet pan from circa 1962 till 1966, and possibly longer.

The headmaster was Mr Slater. In manner and appearance, he was, I recollect, a cross between Wackford Squeers, the school teacher from Charles Dickens' novel, *Nicholas Nickleby* – for he was a Yorkshireman and (sometimes) wielded a cane – and Nikita Khrushchev, as he was small and bald. He retired while I was at Mill Road in 1965, so he was probably born about 1900 and probably learned his craft as a teacher in the early '20s from teachers whose careers very likely encompassed the later years of Victoria's reign. To us he was rather gruff and austere. If he encountered a child who had been expelled from the classroom to stand in the corridor, he would return the child to the room with a spank on the bottom. Corporal punishment was an everyday part of school life but restricted to men and boys. Some – though not all – male teachers kept a cane in their classroom and these were thin, pliable and straight; they did not have a curved handle. One young teacher, Mr 'Pop' Marshall – who, as his nickname suggested, was universally popular and something of a character – had a cane as thick as an old broom handle, although this was very probably more of a 'psychological weapon' than an actual one. The women teachers never used canes and no girls were ever subject to a caning.

I was caned just once. On one day in my first or second year, our class was in the hands of an elderly semi-retired supply teacher, Mr Fitzpatrick, who was covering for our usual teacher. At the start of the lesson, he declared there was to be a rule of silence that, if broken, he warned, would result in a caning. Some minutes later, having made a mistake in pencil, I whispered across to another boy to borrow his rubber. Immediately I was called to the front and told to put out an outstretched hand and the cane came thrashing down with a sharp sting on my palm. I remember clearly not so much the pain, but my sense of injustice, for I had simply whispered an urgent

Class 8 at Mill Road School, Higher Bebington, summer 1963. David, wearing the school tie, is seated second row, second from the left. Linda Shorrock is standing, third row, extreme left. The class teacher is Miss Crosswaite and to her left is Mr Fitzpatrick who was not afraid to use the cane.

'work-related' request and was not chattering or making a noise. The class continued to the end in deathly silence. Mr Fitzpatrick, incidentally, was the only teacher I ever recall who had a coal fire lit in the classroom grate.

On that particular day, our usual teacher in that first year, Miss Crosswaite, a young Lancashire woman, must have been absent. She, however, did not need a cane. She was strict and serious and brooked no nonsense: a mere look was enough to bring the class or any individual to order. In those days a whole school year seemed like an epoch of one's life, and a school year in one classroom with the one teacher for nearly the entire time became a way of life. But one epoch is replaced by another and our second year began with a new teacher, Miss Ball. She was the sister of Alan Ball, the footballer, who at the time played for Blackpool but was later to become famous as a player for Everton and England. At Christmas, we decorated the classroom – as was customary – with lots of coloured paper chains that were festooned across the ceiling. Miss Ball brought into a school a nativity scene made from a hollowed out gnarled root of an old tree, inhabited with tiny figures representing Mary and Joseph, the baby Jesus in his manger, and other figures

– doubtless the shepherds and the three wise men, or were they kings? It had been made by her father or grandfather. The interior was lit by a hidden light bulb and aged 8 I found this quite magical. Miss Ball left before the 'epoch' had run its course and for the rest of the second year our teacher was an energetic young man – from Wales, I think – called Mr Boyce. He was to become one of the best teachers I ever had: encouraging, interested and positive.

My school reports survive, and it is clear from these that Mr Slater was a conscientious head teacher – with impeccable handwriting – who took a close interest in all his pupils. When we were about 8, he taught us how to do 'joined up' or 'double' writing. For this we were supplied with special lined paper with two top lines: one to mark the height of the capital letters and then another line to ensure the lower-case letters were of a consistent size and form. The script was copperplate and thus took a forward slant. Some of the capitals were quite elaborate and difficult to master. The capital letter 'Q', I thought, was rather surprising as it looked very much like a number '2' and some of the others, with their loops and scrolls, required a confident hand.

We were supplied with ugly grey ball-point pens – school issue with no lids – but I soon started experimenting with fountain pens. Our desks – which I thought looked old-fashioned even at 7 or 8 – were made with a recess at the top for an ink well. I got hold of a white ceramic ink pot from the classroom cupboard that fitted the hole and for the rest of my school days I made a terrible mess with Quink, Stephenson's or Parker blue ink. I spilled it on the desk, on my work – doubtless on my clothes – and for the next few years during term time my index and middle fingers of my right hand were perpetually ink stained, in royal blue. The desks combined a bench seat and desk joined by a cast-iron frame. We always occupied the same desk and the sloping desktop was a lid hinged at the top that enclosed a storage space, large enough for exercise books, perhaps a book or two from the classroom library and our own stuff.

We doubtless applied our new-found skills as copperplate scribes in writing and in my second year at junior school we kept a 'news book' of current events – of time moving forward. I recorded the Great Train Robbery – presumably at the beginning of the 1963 autumn term – as the robbery had taken place during the summer holidays. It has often been said over the years that people can remember exactly what they were doing the moment that President John F. Kennedy was assassinated. I am one of those people. It was the evening of 22

November 1963. We had just finished our evening meal – which we always called 'tea'. I was sitting at the pale blue kitchen table drawing or painting. My mum suddenly came into the kitchen visibly shaken and upset and said that Kennedy had been assassinated. I'm not sure that I knew much about who Kennedy was until that moment, but my mum's shock and grief conveyed the awfulness of this news. So, I was concerned too and quickly learned of the events of that day in Dallas, Texas, when the President of the United States was shot and killed, allegedly by Lee Harvey Oswald, whilst riding in an open-top car with his wife, the First Lady Jacqueline Kennedy.

A sharper awareness of who was who in British politics dates from about this time. I remember hearing frequently the names Christine Keeler and Khrushchev on the radio news without understanding the news stories. I don't think I was ever fully aware that Harold Macmillan was the Prime Minister until he was replaced by Alec Douglas-Home. Nor do I have any recollection of Hugh Gaitskell, the Labour leader, but I have a clear memory of seeing a straw poll on early evening television news that must have been shortly after his death in early 1963 when people in the street were shown pictures of Harold Wilson and George Brown and asked whom they preferred. Harold Wilson, of course, won the leadership contest and then the following year narrowly beat the Conservatives in the General Election, ending as he used to say – tobacco pipe in his hand – 'thirteen years of Tory misrule'. I have a clearer recollection of the 1966 General Election, which took place in my last year at Mill Road. One day during the election campaign on my way home from school for lunch I bumped into the MP for Bebington, Geoffrey Howe, in Well Lane near our house. Wearing a large blue rosette, he gave me a lapel pin badge – blue, of course – bearing the slogan, 'For Bebington Howe Now'. He was very nice and approachable, I thought, and he asked me if I would promise to wear it until the election. Bashfully, I said yes, but it did not save Howe from losing his seat to Labour: nationally Labour spectacularly increased their lead.

Back in the classroom, arithmetic was another major strand of junior school life – and for me, one of its less enjoyable aspects. It involved number crunching long multiplication or long division of pre-decimal sums of money. Dividing £8 13s 8½d by – say 12 – was quite tedious as the pounds first had to be converted to shillings and then the shillings carried over added to the 13 shillings and these, in turn converted to pennies, mindful that there were 240 pence in one pound. We learned our times tables by a clock method. This employed a clock dial numbered one to twelve in the usual way with the numbers two to twelve, each in turn, placed in the centre of the dial. So, with a seven in the centre and the one hand placed at seven, the class would shout out 'forty-nine'; with a twelve in the centre and the hand set to eight, we would shout out 'ninety-six'. And so on. I was rather good at this – nine nines? – and my hand would be the first to shoot up and I would call out 'eighty-one' without hesitation. Unfortunately, as I later reflected, this method simply proved that I was good at learning by rote – and that I had a good memory. But it did not further my understanding of basic mathematics and for a while I had difficulty accepting that one multiplied by one could be one. I saw multiplication as a faster way of increasing numbers than by adding them together; so if one plus one is two, surely I thought, one times one had to be just that little bit more …

I was better at art than arithmetic and from about the age of 7 or 8 drew and painted endlessly. In this my mother was very encouraging. She saw this as an aptitude inherited from my architect grandfather and when I was about 8 I was given for Christmas a Windsor and Newton watercolour paint box that consisted of a black tinned iron box with a compartment at the front for two or three paintbrushes and about sixteen little white plastic inserts containing tablets of colours such as viridian green, cobalt blue and burnt sienna. Anything that interested me – or that I thought looked nice – I wanted to draw, so there was a strong aesthetic impulse in my interests and when I was about 8 I liked the look of fighting ships of the time of the Spanish Armada, pirates, cavaliers and drew them endlessly – along with steam trains, of course.

I also became interested in some of the older things around me such as old-fashioned fireplaces, matchboxes and candles – old pens and ink bottles – old-fashioned water pumps and taps and Victorian street lamps. At the same time, I began to hate things made of plastic – to me they were soulless and without character and thus seemed to typify the dreary suburban world we lived in. So many of our everyday household things were made of plastic – the washing-up bowl, the soap tray, buckets and brushes, ballpoint pens and some of our toys. If we joined the two boys next door, Brian and John, for lunch we used to eat a simple meal of tinned soup or macaroni cheese from slightly faded red plastic bowls. Little did I think, however, that fifty years on, waste plastic would constitute such a major environmental disaster.

On my ninth birthday – or a day or two later – I drew a cross section of a brick lean-to building on the back of an envelope. It contained some of the things I liked. The structure has a tiled roof and a coal-burning grate and

A brick lean-to with a large coal fire burning on a grate, drawn by David on the back of a birthday card envelope, 20 June 1964. The idea was that some of the smoke from the fire was piped under a greenhouse shown on the left to provide heat. Candles and boxes of matches are on the shelf behind the fire and below is a cellar with a dripping tap, logs, a barrel and sack of coal.

chimney. There are matchboxes and candles on a shelf and a man in a waistcoat and flat cap smoking a pipe and standing arms akimbo on a pile of coal. There are logs and coal stored in a cellar, which has a dripping tap and more coal heaped up in the cramped loft space, which is lit by a single candle. I drew a dog-legged iron pipe that drew the heat and smoke from the fire to a void under a greenhouse on the left to provide underfloor heating. Outside it is raining. The following month I made my first attempt to draw in perspective by adding a side elevation with receding lines. I still have this first effort – a drawing of a church – although the receding lines were a bit random, with the result that the drawing is more Picasso than Piranesi. Another trick I discovered around this time was using the side of a sharp pencil to create shading.

When I was probably in my second year at junior school, my mother gave me a set of old cigarette cards featuring the kings and queens of England, which had belonged to my grandfather, Fred, who had smoked for much of his life. Actually, I discovered, there were two sets: the older one, printed for WD and HO Wills, only went up to Victoria, and her regnal dates were left open, so these cards clearly dated from earlier than 1901 when she died. The second set came from packets of Players cigarettes and came from the 1930s, for they included King Edward VII, George V and Queen Mary. This second set was printed in brighter colours than the earlier cards. Sorting through these and putting them in order was an excellent way of learning the dates of the reigns of English kings and queens from the time of King Alfred. It further heightened my interest in and understanding of time, and now with dates going the other way, backwards.

On these old cigarette cards, the faces of fierce Saxon kings – plus the odd Dane – stared back at me; then there were murderous monarchs such as King Richard III, monarchs like Henry VIII and Queen Elizabeth who readily beheaded their enemies – which included wives, great aunts and cousins – and then another king who was beheaded himself. Having struggled with my reading up to the age of 6 or 7, I was now an avid reader and began to 'hoover up' information from history books in the classroom, including *The Adventure from History* series published by Ladybird books. Through these books I acquired a fascination with history, particularly from the reign of Elizabeth I (1558–1603) to around the mid-eighteenth century. Some of the words and pictures of the Ladybird books have stayed with me a lifetime, like the description of a super cool Sir Francis Drake intent on finishing his game of bowls before defeating the Spanish Armada. I had my own copies of the Ladybird books of Elizabeth I, Sir Walter Raleigh and Oliver Cromwell; in my 1964 diary, I recorded the purchase of the Ladybird *Story of Captain Cook* on 7 March.

Through the Ladybird books, Charles II became my hero. His was a romantic and irresistible story: a loyal son to his father, the late Charles I, fighting for the royal cause against Oliver Cromwell's troops at the Battle of Worcester. Which he lost. A fugitive on the run, he hid from Cromwell's Ironsides in an oak tree, the famous Royal Oak at Boscobel (providing the name for hundreds of future English inns and public houses, including the pub in Higher Bebington village). Then, after almost a decade of abject poverty as a refugee on the Continent, he was 'Restored'. The Restoration is beautifully illustrated in the book. King Charles, sporting long black hair (or a full-bottomed wig) and dressed in expensive and colourful clothes, is welcomed back by loyal and cheering subjects; they had tired of Christmas being cancelled by the Puritans and wished for the political stability that came with a monarchy backed by Parliament – and not the army. I learned of the Great Plague of London in 1665 and the Great Fire the following year. The book steers clear of the dissolute life of the Restoration Court – the string of royal mistresses, including Nell Gwynne – and casts King Charles as a good king and a good man. The last paragraph of this book, written by Laurence Du Garde Peach (1890–1974), and first published in 1960, pays tribute to the King with these words: '... perhaps what made him most popular was that he was gay ... a king who loved music and singing and dancing, and all gay and happy things, was certain to be liked.'

A generous epitaph, and a startling illustration of how the meaning of some words can change so fundamentally within a few decades.

Another source of interest and inspiration were the old Puffin Picture Books, first published during the war, which had belonged to my mother when she was young. My two favourites, *Village and Town* and *Trees in Britain*, were illustrated by Stanley R. Badmin (1906–89). Both had a strong historical angle. The book on trees showed the deciduous ones in summer and winter. I learned a lot from this book about the different shapes of our trees and from an early age understood that the timber of each tree had its own properties that determined its traditional uses: oak for timbered houses, furniture and gates, sycamore for butter pats and rolling pins and willow for basket work and cricket bats. It is, besides, a beautiful book and I used to seek inspiration from its pages when drawing and painting. *Village and Town* taught me to understand the basics of architectural styles and how they evolved over the centuries, and also the importance of the underlying geology in determining building materials and local styles of architecture (I only learned the word 'vernacular' much later). Looking at this book, my mother used to tell me about how my architect grandfather revered the symmetrical proportions of Georgian architecture and particularly how the proportions of the windows were carefully worked out. So, I grew up believing in the superiority of Georgian architecture over all other styles and saw examples in Rodney Street in Liverpool and Hamilton Square in Birkenhead.

Television also shaped my growing interest in history. A serialisation on TV of the story of Lorna Doone in 1963 made a big impression on me. This introduced me to cannons, muskets and pistols, and through this and the influence of the Ladybird titles my history came to be filled with galleons and other sailing ships, buccaneers, cannons, flintlock muskets and pistols and red coat soldiers with tricornered hats. At that time, I had no interest in twentieth-century history (that was simply yesterday's current affairs, I thought) and neither was I quite so taken with early or medieval history – although I was impressed with a showing on TV of the film *Richard III* on Good Friday 1964; staring Lawrence Olivier, this film exposed the murderous intentions and tortured conscience of Richard 'Crookback' – and memorably his violent end at the Battle of Bosworth Field in 1485.

There were other ways my fascination with the past grew. From around 1964 my parents arranged the delivery of *Look and Learn*, an educational magazine for children: it came with the paper every Monday morning. Frankly, I would have probably preferred a comic like the *Beano*, *Dandy* or *Topper*. Nevertheless, I enjoyed the weekly serialisation of British history that progressed chronologically, reign by reign, and each article was accompanied by an impressive colour illustration. Then there was history to be found underfoot, quite literally, in our garden, which had once been the dumping ground for unwanted stuff from Elm House thrown over the fence. We found bits of blue and white pottery and the remains of one or two hobnailed boots. I found an old-fashioned clay marble, but the most interesting find was a brown earthenware salt cellar. This was almost intact with just a few chips around its flared base. I later recognised this as a piece of stoneware. It was very probably nineteenth century – and very attractive – and for several years I had it as an ornament in my garden. Our house plot had once formed part of an orchard reached from Village Road, which in the past locals must have walked through: Dad found a silver shilling from the reign of George II when digging his vegetable plot at the side of the house. Such finds suggested the ghosts of people from the past – real people – men, women and children going about their everyday lives on the same patch of land that was now our home. This stimulated a curiosity of what our world of Higher Bebington was like over 100 years ago. This was not the history of kings and queens, of major events and heroes like Sir Francis Drake, but of ordinary people, local happenings and commonplace things. These finds and reflections in our back garden sowed the seeds of a lifelong interest in social history – and particularly the history of everyday life.

6

Train Journeys

The very first book I ever purchased was the *Observer's Book of Railway Locomotives*. I ordered it from Mr Wood, the newsagent in Village Road, in February 1964 when I was 8. It cost five shillings and I saved this sum from my weekly spending money. My fascination with railways had started early. In 178 my bedroom window looked out from the back of the house over a wide expanse of public park, a cemetery and then a line of trees in the direction of Lower Bebington. In the distance the presence of trains passing on the main line between Birkenhead and Chester was betrayed by white steam and smoke rising beyond the trees in regular and rapid puffs. I couldn't see the trains, just the puffs of smoke moving briskly from right to left – and left to right – but when we travelled by bus to shop in Lower Bebington in the late 1950s, I used to beg Mum to stay on the bus an extra stop so we would see this same stretch of line as it passed over a railway bridge at Bebington station. Sometimes I was in luck and as we got off the bus I would see a steam train rushing along the embankment and over the bridge into the station.

When I stayed with Ann Chadwick in May 1959 she used to take me with her when she went shopping in Chester. We used to travel by train and I have a vivid memory of looking down on the trains from a footbridge just beyond the platforms at Chester General station. There were trains coming and going every few minutes. I was incredibly excited. Chester was always a busy station. Then from the late 1950s and into the early '60s, about twice a year, my dad used to take me with him when he visited his family in the West Riding of Yorkshire. I loved my stays at my grandma's house, but the highlight of the trips were the journeys by train from Liverpool Exchange to Halifax and return. As a result, Yorkshire became inextricably linked in my mind with railways and trains of red coaches drawn by black steam engines.

A journey by steam train was an immersive, sensory experience that blended sights, sounds and smells in a unique way that today's heritage steam railways can only partially capture. Steam trains did not slip away unnoticed from stations as diesel and electric trains do today but announced their departure with an explosive blast of exhaust; a moment later, there was a second blast, then a third followed by others, gradually following in quicker succession, as the engine slowly drew its train forward. I was riveted by this sound. Thick, black, coaly smoke, smuts and steam flew from the locomotive chimney, and a whiff of this would enter our coach. As the train drew clear of the platform, there was all the paraphernalia of a busy railway line: signal boxes and signals; a glimpse, perhaps, of a locomotive depot with grimy black engines, waiting their next turn and leaking the odd wisp of steam; bridges, sidings with coaches – some of them old and faded – trucks and other trains and more locomotives. I would settle down for the journey in a mood of quiet excitement and contentment, looking abstractedly out at the rapidly changing view from the coach window as the train accelerated, of streets, factories and the back yards and gardens of houses with washing hanging out to dry.

Once underway, our coach made a mesmerising sound as its wheels passed over the joints in the track. This was something like, 'tucca-t-t', which turned to a rapid sing-song like, 'tucca-t-ta, tucca t-tee, tucca-t-ta, tucca-t-tee' as the train gathered speed. As the coaches began to sing and sway to this rhythmical sound, another marker of speed, especially in open country, was the almost hypnotic rising and lowering of the telegraph wires, every second or so, depending on the speed, from one telegraph pole to the next. Then the tucca-t-ta, tucca-t-tee' would be occasionally interrupted by a loud 'whoosh' as the train passed under a bridge at speed or a brief clatter as the train hurtled at speed over points. These are all sights and sounds that have largely disappeared from today's railway travel. The modern, air-conditioned and hermetically sealed railway coaches dull all exterior sounds, the track is continuous and not jointed, and whilst a preserved steam railway can reproduce much of the authentic experience, it cannot, alas, reproduce the sights and sounds that went with travelling by steam at speed.

I first made these journeys in the late 1950s and gradually got to know some of the station names as our train made its way eastwards into Yorkshire: Wigan, Manchester Exchange and Victoria, Rochdale and Sowerby Bridge. At Manchester, heading east, the train entered Exchange station and left by

Victoria. They were two separate stations once belonging to two separate companies but joined by one long platform – which I learned was the longest in the country. But as a child, from the window of our coach this was just one huge and very busy through station, in continuous action as trains and light engines came and went; this was always a highlight of the journey.

Our route was one of the principal lines of the former Lancashire and Yorkshire Railway that, having crossed the relatively flat terrain of south Lancashire, swung northwards after leaving Manchester and climbed towards Rochdale. A few miles after leaving Rochdale, the train entered Summit Tunnel, one of the oldest railway tunnels in Britain. Built under the guidance of the famous railway engineer George Stephenson (1781–1848), and opened in 1841, this was at the time, at 2,885 yards, the longest railway tunnel in the country.

This piece of early Victorian civil engineering made a big impression on me. Travelling eastwards towards Yorkshire, the train entered the tunnel in Lancashire, where houses were built of red brick and fields bounded by hedges. The tunnel was long and the train clattered noisily through the tunnel bore, the coaches dimly lit by the electric lights and the exhaust of the locomotive ever more audible. The train emerged into daylight only to pass through two more short tunnels. And then we were in Yorkshire, in the rugged landscape of the Yorkshire highlands. Red brick had given way to soot blackened millstone grit, hedges to dry stone walls. It was a startling transformation. Yorkshire was not simply another English county but a world apart; doubtless, many proud natives of Yorkshire would agree.

Our train continued its way eastwards in the narrow valley of the fast-flowing River Calder. I remember clearly my dad pointing it out for he was on his way home. His mother was born Elizabeth Earnshaw in Shipley, north of Bradford in 1890, but her mother, Ellen Ogden, came from the small village of Stanbury above Haworth. Ellen had married a Frank Earnshaw. This was Brontë country and Emily Brontë's Heathcliff was an Earnshaw; perhaps his mercurial character was based on someone in my grandmother's family. It is said that Frank Earnshaw was a volatile and hard-drinking man. Well, so goes the family oral tradition. His daughter, Elizabeth Earnshaw, was a pretty and petite brunette and she married my grandfather, Wilfred Eveleigh, in 1915. He was a shoe maker and repairer and had a fine tenor voice, whilst Elizabeth, in her spare time, was a singer and dancer who went by the name of 'Cissy Earnshaw, the Dainty Soubrette'. They performed as part of a troupe of singers and dancers on the stage in Bradford before the Great War – and doubtless that was how they met.

Eveleigh is not a Yorkshire name. It originates from Devon and is quite common in Exeter. The story I was told as a boy was that my dad's grandfather, Charles Eveleigh, as an old man living in Bradford, would tell my father of his boyhood in Wellington in Somerset. I later established that he was born in 1856 and there was something Thomas Hardy-like in his recollections of putting his head, as a young boy, under the cider press to catch the drips of new cider. His father, Samuel, came from Cullompton in Devon and according to the 1841 census return (which I checked many years later) was a handloom weaver. He was born about 1819 and apparently played the double bass in the church band. Charles played the violin. But in the 1870s there appears to have been a mass migration of woollen workers from Wellington – and perhaps other places on the Devon–Somerset border – to Bradford where, doubtless, opportunities for work in the town's woollen mills offered higher wages with the added bonus of the buzz of town life. This branch of the Eveleighs were part of this northward drift and relocated from Wellington to Little Horton parish in Bradford in the late 1870s. Wilfred was born in Bradford in 1889 and so was his son, Sydney, my father, in 1925. So, this was why my dad could see the River Calder and think he was almost home.

By the time the train passed Todmorden and Hebden Bridge on a falling gradient, it was often early evening and as the landscape merged into darkness, lights dotted the landscape, marking the location of scattered moorland farmsteads. Close at hand, the train hugged the River Calder, the Rochdale Canal and the road in the valley bottom. There were rows of terraced housing – all of a sooty millstone grit, slate or stone roofs and purple-brown glazed chimney pots, large factories and textile mills with tall chimneys. The number of mill chimneys was quite striking. Nearly everything was built of stone, nothing looked out of place and the stone harmonised with the moorland setting. I have always found this a very compelling landscape, even though nowadays most of the tall chimneys have gone, as have many of the mills, whilst virtually all the terraced houses have lost their wooden sash windows and many chimneys have been capped or removed altogether, the glazed chimney pots sadly lost to the skyline.

As the train clattered on through the valley further eastwards – passing through more tunnels and over the odd bridge or viaduct, it passed through

Mytholmroyd, Luddendfoot and Sowerby Bridge. I don't remember much of the last leg of the journey. My paternal grandparents lived high up on the Pennines at 9 Inghead Terrace, Shelf, roughly halfway between Halifax and Bradford. From Halifax, we made our way to Shelf by bus. My grandma always greeted us with a smiling welcome in a strong Yorkshire accent. She typically wore a navy blue dress with large white spots, had crinkly black hair and glasses. Her house was also welcoming with a distinctive homely smell, a blend of pipe tobacco, coal fires and bacon and egg. There was always a bottled beer for my dad – Newcastle Brown – and sometimes a bottle of tomato juice for me. All grandmas, I presumed, had cupboards or half cellars filled with booze. Sleepily, I went to bed in a bedroom at the front. There was a chamber pot under the bed. As I drifted off to sleep, beams of light from car headlights momentarily shone through the curtains, lighting up the room. The moorland scenery, the Yorkshire voices and the distinctive smells of my grandma's home underlined that this was a very different world from 178 and 1 Orchard Way.

Wilfred and Elizabeth Eveleigh with their first-born daughter, Winnifred, c 1916.

Left: 9 Inghead Terrace, Shelf, West Yorkshire, c 1935 with Mavis Eveleigh (born 1919). The sign above the door reads, 'High Class Boot Maker and Repairer'. Right: Sydney Eveleigh (1925-2015) on a metallurgy course at Sheffield University in 1960. One of the tutors was the well-known writer on locomotive history, Dr Bill Tuplin, (1902-75) who was born in Birkenhead.

Inghead Terrace was – and is – a short terrace of millstone grit houses on a main road built in the 1930s with bay windows to the living room and a small front garden behind a low stone wall; number nine was the end house on the right. This was an open home. People – family – came and went and described me as 'our David' – or 'our Syd's Son'. I felt I belonged. I remember my Auntie Winnifred, my father's oldest sister, staying over one night and sharing my bed. I thought that was quite natural. But this was not a straight-forward household. If my grandparents' romance had peaked in January 1915 when they married, it had definitely gone off the boil long before I appeared. My paternal grandparents lived – I learned later – virtually separate lives. I only recall seeing my grandfather once: I have a very tenuous recollection of passing an old man on the landing and someone saying, 'That's your grand-father'. I think I was a little puzzled, if only because I had assumed that the man sitting comfortably in front of the kitchen fire, smoking a pipe with his legs stretched out in front of the fender was the man of the house. Perhaps he was. Mr Rogers, the lodger – a gardener by occupation and a very amiable man he was, too. And he probably had every reason to be. And very content.

He was a tall man who wore a collarless shirt, waistcoat and black boots. And I remember his booted feet resting on a stool before the fire. He, I thought, was my grandfather, but his name was Mr Rogers.

The kitchen fire was a tiled grate of the 1930s with a trivet that supported a big black tea kettle. In the corner by the fireplace there was a coal scuttle and I remember that I and my cousin Steven, who was a few years older than me, were allowed to pee into the scuttle. 'It all gors on fi-ya' was my grandma's explanation. This was, indeed, very different to my life in Wirral. But I rather liked it. The front room had a tiled fireplace with a round brass Indian elephant bell on the shallow mantelshelf. Opposite the fireplace there was a dark brown sideboard with a mirror at the back and on top were displayed two carved wooden heads of women with elaborate head dresses. My dad had brought these back from Bali when he was in the Merchant Navy, so they were no more than about ten or twelve years old when I was little, but as an infant I was quite struck by their presence in the room and thought – like my grandmother – that they were very ancient.

My cousin Steven, born in 1952, and his younger sister, Pamela, were the children of my Auntie Mavis, the third of my grandparents' children: Winnifred came first, then Marjory and then Mavis. Sydney, my father, was the youngest by six years but was always closest to Mavis. In the early 1960s, Mavis lived with her husband, Paul Walton, a builder and haulier – and therefore, my Uncle Paul – and her two children in Elland, which was a little further down the Calder Valley. They lived in Catherine Street and when we visited I was fascinated by a tall, sooty, black mill chimney with a very ornate top like a lantern, which towered over the neighbouring houses. I used to look up out of the window and stare and marvel at this chimney that, in retrospect, like so many other industrial stacks, probably drew its inspiration from Florentine towers of the Cinquecento – not that I understood this, of course, in circa 1960.

I loved the Yorkshire landscape, by day and by night. During the day I was struck by how old-fashioned the houses appeared. In the early 1960s the bright exterior paintwork I was used to at home – in mauves, pale blues and yellow – did not appear to have reached the West Riding. Front doors, I clearly remember, were either black, dark brown, tan or green. There were actually more colours on the buses and the variety of Yorkshire bus liveries amazed me as a child. Some were red, the Bradford buses were blue and cream whilst those in Halifax were painted green, orange and cream.

Bradford and Huddersfield also had trolley buses that, like electric trams, took their power from overhead cables above the street; the presence of these was another way in which the region seemed different and slightly old-fashioned. Dad used the local buses to take me with him when he went shopping in Bradford or called on members of his family. In about 1961 or early 1962, we went by bus to Bradford to see my Great Aunt Hilda, the sister of my grandfather, Wilfred Eveleigh. She had never married. Like so many young women of that generation, she had lost the man who would have likely become her husband in the First World War and so she lived with a companion, Emily Sykes, at 1 Ramsey Street in Little Horton. This was at the end of a long Victorian terrace of millstone grit and when we entered I thought the house was old fashioned and a little chilly. Aunt Hilda had untidy black hair and was wearing a thick bright green cardigan, whilst Emily – who was frail and silver haired – was wearing a lighter one of salmon pink. Hilda and Emily were having difficulty lighting a coal fire in the living room grate when we arrived. They threw sugar on the smoulder-ing coals to encourage them to burst into flame, but the fire just smoked dismally without giving off much heat. I remember thinking the interior was a little cheerless: the furniture was old, there was brownish lino on some of the floors and much of the interior was painted a mid-green, which was a popular colour for interior paintwork in the 1930s. Time dragged for me while Dad talked to the two old ladies for an hour or two, doubtless about his new life in Wirral, his job, our new house and his family. When it was time to go, Auntie Hilda gave me a silver shilling – an old silver one, I remember – from the reign of George V. I never saw her again as she died shortly afterwards. I learned later that this had been the family home for over sixty years from the early 1900s. My great grandfather, Charles, had lived there until his death in early 1947: apparently the Eveleighs had been the first in the terrace to put a bathroom in the house.

At night Yorkshire became a wide expanse of dark hills and moorland with clusters of distant lights visible in every direction, like twinkling constella-tions of stars, marking out the location of towns such as Bradford, Halifax and Elland. I loved the names too: Heckmondwike, Hipperholme, Northorwram (and Southowram), Laisterdyke, Wyke, Brighouse and Cleckheaton. These were names that tripped off my father's tongue when he spoke. They are hard, guttural and unmistakably Yorkshire, and I suspect have a strong Nordic origin. Then it was time to go home. When I was about 3 or 4, I remember waiting for the train on the platform at Halifax station and being unable to control my terror when our train, headed by a large black steam locomotive, suddenly hurtled into the station and ran along our platform at some speed. I couldn't look and buried my head in the platform bench. Then we were home again. But my mother had to face the reality that the little infant son who returned was half-Yorkshire. And she did not like it.

One day we turned up at Liverpool Exchange station to continue our journey to Yorkshire but in place of the usual steam train, there in our platform, to my horror and dismay, was a diesel train of three green coaches. In railway parlance this was a diesel multiple unit, or DMU. When we entered the coach and when I saw the row of low seats, I thought this was more like a bus than a 'proper' train. My disappointment was boundless. This must have been our first journey of 1962 as the trains on this service were dieselised from the end of 1961. The appearance of this diesel train brought home to me the reality that the days of steam were numbered.

In 1955, the year I was born, the British Transport Commission published its Modernisation Plan, which laid out an ambitious programme of investment involving the replacement of steam by diesel and electric by 1970. My dad explained to me that steam locomotives were going to be replaced by diesels. He was also sad and filled with regret. I remember one day, probably in 1963, at Liverpool Exchange when we were about to board our three-coach diesel multiple unit for Yorkshire, standing on its own in the neighbouring platform was a large green steam locomotive, slightly work stained and dusty but nevertheless, impressive. I looked at its huge wheels and the various oiled connecting rods and valve gear that made up the 'motion'. My father saw beauty – a combination of aesthetics and mathematics, no doubt – in the Walschaerts valve gear, which he pointed out to me, for he was a chartered engineer and member of the Institution of Mechanical Engineers. The engine very likely had a name over the middle splasher, but I have no recollection of this. Anyway, I was anxious that we got a good seat on our green 'bus' and so I pulled Dad away and we boarded our train to Halifax.

My interest in railways was less technical than my father's and I would thumb through the pages of my *Observer's Book of Locomotives* and read that the numbers of some classes of steam engines were thinned through withdrawals and scrapping. Against some locomotives types, the author had depressingly noted, 'very few now remain'. However, there were still quite

A train waits impatiently for the off at platform 2 of Birkenhead Woodside on 19 February 1960. The engine's safety valve is lifting, and the fireman appears to be using the steam injector to put water in the boiler and quieten the engine whilst in the station. The trains to Barmouth in 1962 and 1963 were very likely pulled by this type of locomotive as far as Chester.

a few classes of locomotives listed in the book, and therefore still in regular service in 1963 and 1964, which had been designed and built before 1900: such were the steam engines used, for example, for all the services on the Isle of Wight, which dated to the 1890s. Incredibly, my *Observer's Book* included a couple of small tank engines (known as 'Terriers'), still in revenue service in 1963, which had been built at Brighton by the London, Brighton and South Coast Railway in 1872 when William Ewart Gladstone was prime minister! They continued in use on passenger trains between Havant and Hayling Island in Hampshire until later that year. There were other loco-motives dating to the 1880s still at work in other parts of Britain in 1963. This was just one small way in which the Victorian age remained a part of everyday life – for just a little while longer – in the mid-1960s.

On a sunny day in the spring or early summer of 1962 I was in the front garden when Dad told me that we were going to Barmouth in Wales for a holiday and that meant travelling on a train pulled by a locomotive of the

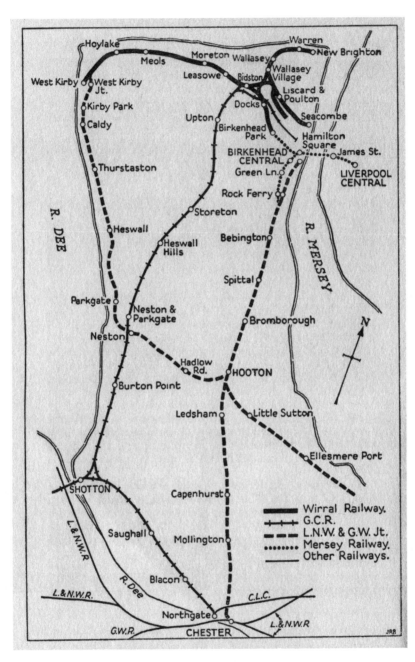

The Wirral peninsular from Campbell Highet, The Wirral Railway, first published in 1961. At 9/- this book was eminently affordable and David purchased a copy in c. 1969. The map shows the railways of the Wirral before closures set in after 1960.

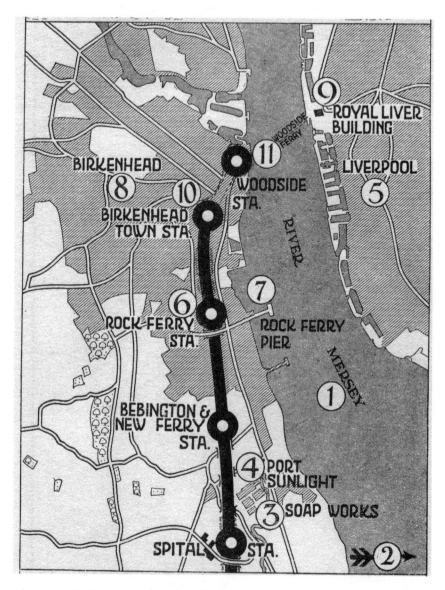

This map of 1925 shows the final lap from Spital and Port Sunlight of the 210½ mile train journey from London Paddington to Birkenhead Woodside by the Great Western Railway. From *Through the Window, Paddington to Birkenhead*, published by the Great Western Railway.

Great Western Railway. He explained to me that locomotives of this company were green and had copper-capped chimneys, brass domes (or safety valve covers), and that some were named after kings or castles, halls, counties, granges or manors. It was to be our first family summer holiday with the promise – for the first time – of going to the seaside.

On a Saturday morning in mid-July we began our journey from home in a large black taxi smelling powerfully of soft old leather upholstery, bound for Birkenhead Woodside station. On arriving, our train was in Platform 2. It consisted of five coaches and one or two freight vans, and was very likely a summer timetable, Saturdays only, direct train from Birkenhead to Barmouth. I was not impressed that our train included goods vehicles: they made the train look rather humble, I thought. Neither was there a gleaming Great Western locomotive at the front of the train, just the usual grimy black engine toned down to a sooty grey.

Then we were off. Immediately we left the platform end and with the usual terrific bark from the exhaust and smoke swirling around us, we entered a tunnel as the train made its way under the streets of Birkenhead. In the gloomy semi-darkness of the compartment we looked at each other in silence as the train climbed noisily through the tunnel. There was just a dull yellow glow from the small electric lamps above the seats. Then suddenly we were back in daylight. There were tracks on both sides: we passed a locomotive depot and coach sidings and then, gathering speed, through Rock Ferry, which was the southerly terminus for the green electric trains that went under the Mersey to Liverpool. Shortly afterwards, we all looked over to our right to see if we could see Higher Bebington and, sure enough, we spotted the spire of our local church and the tower of the windmill on the skyline. We then passed our own station – Bebington – without stopping and continued our way to Chester, passing through Port Sunlight, Spital and Bromborough …

As our train arrived at Chester General, a few train spotters on the platform turned briefly to look at our train but moments later their attention was taken by a more important looking arrival that drew in on our left: a locomotive with a long train of smart-looking dark red coaches; all the spotters – perhaps a dozen or more in number – rushed over to take a closer look. It was probably a summer holiday train – most likely on its way to the North Wales Coast from Leeds or Manchester pulled by a larger and more interesting locomotive than ours. I had to accept that our train was not very remarkable. When we had got on the train at Birkenhead, I almost certainly made sure that I had the 'best' seat, by the window, facing the direction of travel, but at Chester General I was always taken by surprise by the change of engine; the replacement was always coupled to the other end of the train, so when we left the station I now faced the wrong way with my back to the engine.

The train continued at a respectable speed until we reached Llangollen, where I learned a new word: Eisteddfod. In the station, the River Dee rushed and tumbled over the shallows immediately to our left and bunting fluttered above us as part of the festivities marking the town's annual International Eisteddfod. After Llangollen, the train began to drag and progress seemed interminable. The train crawled along. Will it ever go faster, I thought? I became bored and rather fed up. We passed Lake Bala and then, after Dolgellau, the train at last gathered speed. My spirits rallied and then I saw the coast, or more particularly the estuary of the River Mawddach. From the coach window I looked down on perfect yellow sand on a deserted water's edge. I thought this was the beach I would be exploring and playing on tomorrow. But the train clattered onwards with a steady 'tucca-t-t', eventually crossing the river estuary at Barmouth Bridge before drawing up in Barmouth station.

We stayed at the Min-y-Mor Hotel, a late-Victorian detached grey stone building slightly to the north of the main part of the town but just across the road from the beach. The railway ran quite close to the back of the hotel. The entrance was in a square tower on the left-hand front corner. It had a wonderful smell that I can only describe as an aroma perhaps particular to old respectable hotels, a blend of mopped stone floors, perhaps, and of furniture polish, clean linen, toast and coffee. There were some large and seemingly very old pieces of dark oak furniture in the foyer: a chest, a high-backed chair and possibly a settle. Dad said they were hundreds of years old. I looked on them with veneration. There was a lovely sunny walled garden to the side of the hotel where I used to play with my two sisters. There were lots of paths between beds of low shrubs to run around and at one end a large white-painted stone or cement seat – or 'throne' – shaped as an opened oyster shell. Many years later, in about 1982, I returned to Barmouth and found this garden in ruins, the oyster seat a wreck. When I next visited in about 2012, all signs of the garden had disappeared under the tarmac of a new car park.

Barmouth was very different to the Wirral and Yorkshire – not just because it was a seaside resort, albeit a quiet one – but because it was Welsh. In the town there were one or two shop window displays featuring traditional Welsh life, I think, with spinning wheels and the (so-called) Welsh national costume on display with its red shawls and black hats. It is strange to reflect that, unlike the national or regional folk costumes of countries like Sweden, Romania or Greece, which apply to both men and women, the Welsh national dress was – and is – gender specific and really only suitable for women over about the age of 80.

The main attraction, of course, was the beach just across the road from the hotel. We spent several sunny afternoons playing by the sea, making large sandcastles – fortified with moats and ramparts – and then watched as they disintegrated against the incoming tide. By then it was usually time to return to the hotel for tea. But there were days when there was no beach: when the tide was in and a stormy westerly wind and overcast skies turned the Irish Sea from a calm deep blue into a menacing grey and foamy white and large waves heaved and crashed into the sea wall; on those days there was little alternative but to walk into the town.

Turning left out of the hotel we walked along the windswept promenade, crossed the railway line by the station, and continued past the shops in the town centre to an area of narrow streets and steps that climbed and twisted up towards the hill overlooking the town. Mum said this part of Barmouth was 'quaint'. This was another new word etched into my vocabulary as we walked, sometimes with rain dripping from our plastic macs and sou'westers, past (quaint) stone cottages, looking down on their low slate roofs, small paned dormer windows, chimney stacks and chimney pots. We continued upwards until we left the town below us and the road turned into a grassy footpath. Here we passed the entrances of two or three small caves in the hillside, which I imagined were home to old hags with spinning wheels, but as a greenish water oozed from one or two of them, then perhaps not. The path climbed further up the hill through an expanse of closely cropped turf with low clumps of gorse, brambles and bracken. Looking the other way towards the coast, often under leaden skies, we could see the town, the railway station and the single-track line that continued northwards towards Harlech; we could also make out our grey stone hotel, standing on its own, and beside it the walled garden.

The following year we repeated the holiday, only this time staying for sixteen days in the Mini-y-Mor. We made the same train journey from

Birkenhead Woodside, leaving this time from Platform 1, which was against the large retaining wall of the station. We changed trains at Chester and caught a train that was hauled by a green Great Western express locomotive. This journey was memorable. It must have easily been the fastest run by steam I ever experienced. I spent some of the journey standing in the window. I was simply too excited to sit down! We had to leave the train when it stopped at Ruabon. Here I was determined to catch the name and number of the engine when we crossed the overbridge. I caught a glimpse of it with its curved nameplate and dark green paintwork as we climbed the steps. But a train like this was not going to wait for us and by the time we reached the other platform it had gone. So, I never knew the identity of this Great Western thoroughbred, I can only guess that it was a Hall, a Grange or most likely a Manor. We then continued our journey on a third train, which plodded slowly through the Welsh hills to Barmouth.

For the next sixteen days I was in steam railway bliss. The line at Barmouth seemed to challenge the notion that the days of steam were numbered. Not one diesel did I see in sixteen days! Every working passenger and freight was steam hauled, many by modern, so-called 'standard' class steam locomotives, built by British Railways in the 1950s, but I remember seeing a grimy Great Western Manor class, *Torquay Manor*, shunting the yard one day when we crossed the footbridge by the station. The line at Barmouth was busy on those summer days. There were often several locomotives to be seen at the station – some with double chimneys (which I thought meant they were faster and more powerful than single-chimney types) and there were always trains passing the back of the hotel, which I could see through the window of the toilet near our room – all facilities were shared in the 1960s.

Barmouth Bridge, which spans the Mawddach estuary, provided an opportunity to see the trains up close. A timber pedestrian footpath ran alongside the single railway track and sometimes we walked the near half mile across the bridge to Morfa Mawddach on the south side. When a train could be seen approaching in the distance, Mum would fuss about the oncoming dirt and smoke and try and shepherd us into a timber shelter to hide from the engine as it passed. But I would ignore her entreaties and defiantly stand out in the open, taking in the sight and smells of coal, steam and hot oil at close quarters as the locomotive slowly went by, clanking and rattling its train, which sometimes consisted of no more than a few goods vans or trucks, over the bridge.

Back home, Dad befriended a retired engine driver around this time in his local pub, the George Hotel. His name was Bert Richards. He was a tall lean man with a bullet head of short cropped grey hair, courteous and polite, who lived in a road off Town Lane in Bebington. He used to come to the house and sit in our kitchen, where he would tell us stories of his working days as an engine driver with the Great Western Railway. We learned that he had been born somewhere near Reading West station around 1900, that he had lied about his age to join the Army during the First World War and had fought in the Battle of Ypres – which he pronounced, 'Why Prez'. His railway stories where full of mishaps involving, I think, runaway trains (or parts of them), wrong signals and the like between Birkenhead, Chester and Shrewsbury, but sadly I cannot remember a single one. How and why he came to Birkenhead I do not know. All I remember is that he thought Great Western engines were the very best and that he ended his days based at Birkenhead Sheds off Mollington Street working the local diesel multiple unit trains to Chester. Knowing my interest in railways, one day he gave me his Great Western Railway *Rule Book*, a dark green clothbound pocket book of 1933, and subsequently, *The General Appendix*, a pale blue paperback of 1936, containing more rules and operating procedures. These were amongst my earliest books and they remain treasured possessions over fifty years on.

The following year, on 4 September 1964, I made my last British Railways journey by steam. Again, we left Birkenhead Woodside for Wales but this time heading for Llandudno along the North Wales coast to visit my great aunts, Gertrude and Lilias, the sisters of my grandfather, Fred, who lived in retirement in a late 1950s bungalow at Rhos-on-Sea, near Colwyn Bay. The interior was filled – like the homes of many older people at that time – with old furniture, Victorian and Edwardian. In the hallway there was an eight-day longcase clock. Its white enamelled face was surmounted by a picturesque representation of the sun and the moon that, in a celestial-like arrangement, was supposed to cross the top of the dial every twelve hours, only the clock wasn't working as the minute hand had snapped off. I remember clearly that throughout the bungalow there was an all-pervasive cloying, musky smell that may have had something to do with mothballs, ladies' scent and furniture polish. Auntie Gertrude was older than my grandfather. She had been born in Liverpool in 1883 and was another palpable link with the Victorian Age. I only saw her that once – she looked terribly old, I thought, with thin, bony hands crossed with thick blue veins. She died the following February and was buried in Smithdown Road Cemetery, Liverpool.

We left my great aunts early evening and caught a return train from Colwyn Bay. I remember admiring the steam locomotive as it rolled into the station with its complement of maroon coaches. I looked at the reciprocating parts of the engine's motion glistening with oil as it came to rest. I turned around to my parents and said the engine was well oiled and looked in good condition. I had expectations for a fast run. We found seats in a compartment coach and were joined by a friendly older man and his wife. He was, he told us, a retired engine driver who used to drive the Emerald Isle Express, a Euston to Holyhead service, along this stretch of line. It was a fine, clear early evening and soon the train was running at quite a speed. I could see the adjacent track rushing by in a blur: the train set up a fast and smooth rhythm over the jointed track, swaying a little and hurrying under bridges and over points as it sprinted towards Chester. Our engine driver companion assured us we were doing well over seventy. I was exhilarated!

We reached Chester at dusk. As we pulled into the station, our coach window drew up alongside a steam locomotive on the adjacent track. It was an indeterminate grimy grey, but it carried the name *Indore* on a curved nameplate over the wheels; this, I thought, was a very odd name for a railway engine. Upon checking the index of locomotive names in my *Observer's Book of Locomotives*, I established that *Indore* was a Jubilee class locomotive and then I subsequently learned that Indore is a city in India. The Jubilees were express engines, first introduced in 1934 with some built in the Jubilee year of 1935. They were named after places in the British Empire and famous admirals of the British Navy, and so under the dirt and grime of neglect, *Indore* carried the green livery of a British Railways express engine. But its days were almost over. It was withdrawn later that month. Some locomotives were more fortunate: in February 1964, I had noted in my diary that *Mallard*, holder of the world steam record of 126mph, which had been withdrawn in April 1963, was going to a museum.

It was dark when our train finally drew into Birkenhead Woodside. As we walked up the platform, the locomotive quickly uncoupled from the train and reversed out of the station. Only a few other passengers left the train. Silence descended over the dimly lit interior. Vaguely aware of the arcaded and ornate brick walls, I looked up at the huge cavernous glazed roof and the large cast iron columns supporting it. The light from the suspended lamps was feeble and the station almost empty. It was an impressive terminus station, but it felt unloved and forlorn. And its days were indeed already numbered. The grim reaper in the form of the Beeching Report, published in 1963, had identified this fine station, opened in 1878, as part of the unprofitable third of the railway network that had to go.

The Reshaping of British Railways, written by Dr Richard Beeching (1913–85) and published by the British Railways Board, aimed at making the railways commercially viable by cutting out the parts of the network that were identified as unprofitable: 5,000 miles of railway line and 2,363 stations were to go in order to stem the large operating losses caused by the inexorable rise of car ownership. For this was the age of the car, of the motorway and the inner-city ring road. Many post-war urban development plans were designed around the assertion that the free and uninterrupted flow of motor traffic in a city centre was a top priority, certainly much higher than the conservation of historic streets and buildings. In the early 1960s the government was also on the side of the car, shamelessly investing in road building in preference to any subsidy for the railways. Trains did not fit the modern and progressive '60s. They were widely regarded as old-fashioned, slow and dirty, but the paradox is that as soon as Beeching's recommendations were published, popular opinion started to swing the other way.

Dr Beeching (1913–85),
Chairman of the British
Railways Board 1961-65

Dr Beeching was vilified. He became famous, or rather infamous, for his 'axe'. He argued his closures amounted to careful surgery, not 'mad chopping', but there was no consideration of the wider economic and social consequences of the proposed closures: this was a case of applying a simple profit and loss analysis to each route. Some lines were clearly hopelessly unprofitable but there was concern that some parts of rural Britain, in the age of the private motor car, were likely to face a new type of isolation, notwithstanding the promise of replacement bus services. There was also a large dose of nostalgia. John Betjeman (1906–84), later Poet Laureate, had led the opposition to the closure of branch lines from the early 1960s, arguing that railways were an essential and much-loved feature of traditional British life along with the parish church and the village pub.

Aged 8, I knew nothing of John Betjeman. I was simply sad that the way of travelling by train that I loved was not going to last forever – and I was never particularly interested in cars. But I clearly remember the song, *Slow Train*, written by Flanders and Swann in 1963. The boys next door, Brian and John, had a copy of the single. I used to go around to their house and listen to the song with its sad rollcall of condemned stations contained in the lyrics. Birkenhead Woodside was one. Some lines and stations condemned by Beeching were ultimately reprieved, but our holiday line from Ruabon through Llangollen towards Barmouth was condemned and closed in early 1965; Birkenhead Woodside lingered on until 5 November 1967.

7

Evenings and Weekends

'Good evening all.' With these words and a salute, PC George Dixon of Dock Green greeted his television audience every Saturday evening on the BBC. Standing in uniform under the light of a blue police lamp, Jack Warner (1895–1981), who played the policeman – the archetypal English Bobby – gave a brief introduction to each episode and then a piece at the end that normally concluded that crime doesn't pay. Television was a major influence in my early years. It entertained, sometimes informed and inspired me, and the TV schedule, published weekly in the *Radio Times*, gave shape and definition to our evenings: 'It's Friday, it's five o'clock … it's *Crackerjack*'. And so, days of the week and times of the evening were defined by the published television programme.

Dixon of Dock Green salutes his television audience.

Evenings began when Children's Hour started at 4.55 p.m., although this was later brought forward to about 4.30 p.m. when *Jackanory*, a story-telling programme for younger children, was introduced. We normally ignored this, so just before 5 p.m., Janet, Helen and I would settle down in the living room, in cold weather with the rattle of the electric poker lighting the fire, and for the next hour or so until the start of the early evening news watch children's television together. BBC television reigned supreme in our house. Watching ITV – the commercial channel – was discouraged by our parents – if not actually banned. With its advertisements for everything from cigars to soap powder and its heavy reliance on American imports, Mum and Dad enforced the idea that ITV was low-brow and brash. We watched it when we could (*Thunderbirds*, for example, was a favourite) but for us, Children's Hour was mostly about the BBC offerings: programmes such as *Animal Magic* with Johnny Morris and *Vision On*, an art programme aimed chiefly at children with impaired hearing, presented by Tony Hart and Pat Keysall, which used a jazzy tune (Left Bank Two by The Noveltones) as background music. Then there were several American imports – shows and cartoons – that I never really liked. However, *Blue Peter* was essential viewing, presented for several years in the 1960s by the famous trio of Valerie Singleton, Christopher Trace (later replaced by Peter Purves) and John Noakes – not forgetting, of course, Petra, the dog. But my very favourite programme was *Tales from Europe* which mostly came from countries behind the Iron Curtain.

I grew up in a world where Europe was split: Western Europe and the Communist Bloc. There was even a sense of the inevitability of a Third World War. It was just a matter of when, and with the dreadful certainty that this war would be nuclear. So, it was something of a miracle that in the midst of the Cold War, children in Britain settled down in front of the television on a Thursday early evening to watch superbly produced films made for children by people who could not freely travel to the West and who were also, quite possibly, our future enemies. Many came from East Germany and two that I remember are *The Singing Ringing Tree* and the *Tinder Box Man*: the first loosely based on a Grimms' fairy tale and the second on the famous story by Hans Christian Andersen. The episodes of *Tales from Europe* were beautiful, strange and magical. Another foreign production of a Hans Christian Andersen story was a cartoon of the story of the Snow Queen. This was apparently a 1957 production from the Soviet Union and a translation was shown a few times in the early and mid-sixties by the BBC as a one-off at Christmas. I remember being slightly scared by the sinister Snow Queen and fascinated by the journey – ever northwards – of Gerda searching for her brother, Kay, who was being held captive by the Snow Queen in her palace of ice in Lapland. These Eastern European productions were, I thought, infinitely more appealing and interesting than the American sitcoms and cartoons such as *Bewitched*, *The Munsters* and *Top Cat* that flooded into our front rooms in the 1960s; by comparison they seemed corny and overtly commercial with the canned laughter prompting the gags.

Other favourites from the BBC were the cartoon *Captain Pugwash* and the comedy *Steptoe and Son*. Very likely the superb acting and pathos of the two rag and bone men – father and son – was lost on me as a boy but I loved the scruffy setting with the yard, the horse and cart and, of course, the parlour filled with junk, including a stuffed bear and even a skeleton. Above all else, I loved the character of Steptoe senior, the way he would grin and grimace, mostly behind his son's back. Another favourite was *Mr Pastry*, which was aired on Saturdays once *Grandstand* was over. I don't remember much in detail of this programme except for Mr Pastry's white moustache, but as an 8-year-old I thought he was very funny. Then in November 1963 – just after Kennedy's assassination – something went terribly wrong: *Mr Pastry* was replaced by *Doctor Who*.

Doctor Who brought fear and misery to my life, yet it was compulsive viewing. I clearly recall the first showing and the first time I heard that theme tune (produced in the BBC's Radiophonic Workshop). It was a momentous event. Everything about *Doctor Who* was unsettling, if not downright scary – including the music, the moving abstract patterns that accompanied it, the sound the Tardis made when 'taking off', and then the Daleks. With time travel the basic ingredient, the first series went back in time to a time of cave dwellers, and the second to the future, to a distant planet where the Daleks had ousted the native population and survivors lived in a marshy jungle. Daleks were seemingly invincible, ruthless destroyers, killing their enemies with a crackling utterance of 'Exterminate' and firing their 'death ray' gun. There had been nothing on television quite like this. It is often said that many children hid behind the sofa when the Daleks appeared. I would have done this if I could, but our settee was against the wall so I used an armchair instead, or more usually hid my eyes behind my fingers and peeped out when I dared.

I would wake up on a Sunday morning half expecting to find a Dalek poking my bedclothes, and I would think there would very likely be one in our garage if I was sent there in the dark to fetch some stored shallots or garlic for our evening meal. That the arm of a Dalek looked rather like Mum's kitchen sink plunger and that a Dalek (at least the original ones of 1963) could not negotiate stairs – or any rough ground – did nothing to reduce my total fear of this robot race. That they had been created and fabricated by the BBC also never crossed my mind. What was real was my fear and dread, and therefore the Daleks were real and capable of popping up anywhere. Strange to say, in recent years, Daleks *have* popped up in all kinds of unexpected places: I have seen them on display in shopping centres, for example, and taking part in street carnivals and museum exhibitions. They now seem so harmless and fully integrated into a diverse and multi-cultural, intergalactic universe. But in 1963, I was resentful that *Mr Pastry* had gone and that my peace had been invaded by these ruthless and terrifying exterminators.

Most of my drawing and watercolour painting was done at home after tea and at weekends in the kitchen, sitting at the pale blue Formica table. In the background, there was the constant chatter of the wireless broadcasting the popular music played on the Light Radio. Everyday life at home in the 1960s took place to the sound of music, not the songs from the 1959 musical and 1965 film – which I have always detested – but the music that played through the day on the radio and in the evening on TV. Mr and Mrs Savage next door had their radio permanently tuned into the BBC's Home Service; my mother, however, preferred the Light Programme. In 1967 these were to become respectively Radio 4 and Radio 2. So, in 1 Orchard Way, popular music provided the background to everyday life.

Popular music covered many styles and, of course, was to change dramatically in the 1960s. It also varied according to the time of day; in other words, according to the programme. During the week there were programmes dedicated to housewives, workers on their lunch break and in the early evening for everyone returning home – that was *Roundabout*. Each was typically introduced by a jaunty, high-tempo orchestral arrangement combining strings, wind and brass with electric guitar and drums in a very '60s style. *Roundabout* was followed by *The Archers*, which was the cue for my parents when I was an infant to instruct me to put my toys away, put on my pyjamas and get ready for bed. Invariably, I had something better to do than go to bed and so the *Archers* theme music (more jaunty strings) filled me with dread, signalling that my day was almost over.

Then it was the weekend. Saturday mornings and the whole weekend stretched ahead. If the weather was fine, the early morning sun streamed through the sycamore and the hawthorn and lit the garden lawn with dappled light. Wood pigeons cooed in the trees: the air was fresh, the day ahead full of promise. These were the best of days, when I would think of the adventures that could unfold through the day. And as I ate my breakfast and anticipated the day ahead, *Children's Favourites* brought a range of popular music for a young audience into our kitchen. There are certain songs that I will always associate with Saturday mornings: *The Laughing Policeman*, for example (sung by Charles Penrose and recorded in 1926), which sounded very old fashioned, even in the early 1960s. Then there were a few I loved, such as Lonnie Donegan's *My Old Man's a Dustman*. This was my first-ever favourite song. I thought the words were hilarious, though I rather doubt if I understood any of the jokes in the lyrics of this song when it was a Number One hit in 1960:

Oh, my old man's a dustman
He wears a dustman's hat
He wears cor blimey trousers
And he lives in a council flat

But there were many tunes I simply tolerated, songs that were simply the musical background to the cornflakes, toast and Robertson's Golden Shred marmalade of a Saturday morning. In this category were *Thank Heaven for Little Girls* by Maurice Chevalier, *Nellie the Elephant* and *Michael Row a Boat Ashore*. And then there was *Good Gracious Me* sung by Peter Sellers and Sophia Loren, which I used to think was somehow, well ... a bit creepy; but my Number One Hate was *There's a Hole in My Bucket*, a hit for Harry Belafonte in 1961. I could never understand how anyone would wish to sit down and choose to listen to that deadpan and turgid dialogue between Henry and Eliza about a defective bucket, let alone go out and buy the record; yet people did, and it was purchased in sufficient quantities to become a UK chart hit. If rock and roll hits by Elvis Presley were ever featured on this programme, then I forget. I suspect they were not. But I am sure that around 1965 songs from the film, *The Sound of Music*, entered the play list. As ghastly memories of Henry's bucket with its hole faded from memory, I acquired a new Number One Hate: *Doe, a Deer, a Female Deer ...*

In the early 1960s, there were several deliveries made on Saturday mornings and most knew to come to the back door. Our Sunday joint of meat was delivered by Parry's, a butcher in Lower Bebington; Mr Stoneleigh, the affable local green grocer in Village Road, came around in his brown cotton twill overall with our order of fruit and vegetables. Then there was the milkman, of course, who made his way around Higher Bebington in his electric milk float. Another daily delivery was the bread man, who knocked on the back kitchen door with a plastic tray of bread and cakes. Mum usually chose Hovis or Allinson's sliced brown bread, sometimes adding a packet of jam tarts to her purchase. We ate prodigious quantities of bread and butter with prodigious quantities of jam, although I was never keen on brown bread and always wished for white. Our usual jam was Robertson's blackcurrant or strawberry jam. I preferred the latter and always tried to dig out the solid sugary strawberries.

The newspapers – along with the weekly *Radio Times* – were delivered by the paper boy and every week the council binmen turned up with their large refuse vehicle. One of the team would lift the galvanised dustbin that lived next to the coal bunker and carry it effortlessly over his shoulder to the vehicle in the road. No one in the 1960s could imagine a world where the corrugated dust bin with its clanging lid would ever give way to plastic wheelie bins, recycling boxes and black bin liners. Other less frequent callers included the coal man, who decanted the contents of several hundred weight hessian sacks into the coal bunker. On summer afternoons, a cream-painted ice cream van would occasionally stop noisily on the corner of Well Lane and Orchard Way with a loud and repetitive tune its trade call; Dad would go out into the road and buy us three children a slice of vanilla ice cream held between two wafers. Later in the decade, probably in response to the wider ownership of cars, the Saturday morning deliveries gradually fell away. Then it was up to us to buy our own provisions and collect the Sunday joint, the bread and the vegetables.

All our immediate needs were supplied by the shops in Higher Bebington. In the 1960s it was usual for every suburb to be self-sufficient with a row or two of mostly independently owned shops that answered for the daily requirements of the immediate neighbourhood. The idea of the 'big shop' done in one go in a large supermarket – or of shopping in a giant indoor mall – were then quite unknown, and the presence of self-service checkouts, pin numbers and contactless credit and debit cards could not have been fore-told. More important shopping – for clothes or furnishings – took us further afield to Birkenhead, Liverpool or Chester but most of our food and other household goods could be obtained just a few minutes' walk from 1 Orchard Way – either in the few shops in Village Road or across the main road on Teehey Lane. The latter was the most important of the two and included a Post Office run by Mr Grundy – his son Kevin was in my class at Mill Road School. There was a Midland Bank at the top of Town Lane, and in the row of 1930s shops on Teehey Lane next to the new Co-op supermarket, there was a chemists', a haberdasher's and drapers, a shoe shop, ladies' hairdresser, an ironmonger, greengrocer and a radio and TV repair shop.

Such shops could be multiplied in their thousands across Britain in the 1950s and '60s, yet as family run enterprises they all had their own particular personality and idiosyncrasies according to the individuals who owned and ran them. The greengrocer's and barber's shop was run by the Harfords, husband and wife. Mr Harford had fought in the Second World War and, I recollect, had learned to cut hair in the Army. The greengrocer's business was at the front facing the main road and run principally by Mrs Harford, whilst Mr Harford carried on his business as a barber in a room at the back and reached through a narrow, dark passage, floored with old-fashioned pat-terned linoleum. At the far end was the barber's shop, where there were two – what seemed to me as a young boy – massive barber's chairs, although only one was ever in use as Mr Harford worked alone, with only his row of waiting customers for company. Whilst waiting for my turn, I used to love looking through the pages of comics like the *Dandy* and the *Beano*, which were piled up on a low table alongside the chairs. These comics were never brought home, so I read the adventures or misadventures of Desperate Dan, The Bash Street Kids or Denis the Menace with relish.

I would normally have my hair cut on a Saturday morning accompanied by my father. While my hair was being cut, Mr Harford would talk to Dad about the ups and downs of Tranmere Rovers; the club's ground at Prenton Park was just over a mile and a half away along the main road. Mr Harford's concentra-tion distracted by his analysis of the Rovers' form, I used to return home, to my mother's consternation, with a lopsided and ragged fringe and very short sides. There was no concept of styling, just cutting. When I was a little older, aged about 9 or 10, I used to go on my own and feel very grown up, walking through the front shop – past the fruit and vegetables – opening the door into the narrow passageway and entering the back room with its two chairs, mirrors and other barbers' stuff. This was very much a man's world, I thought. It had a distinctive smell, probably comprising cigarette smoke, cut hair, lino and hair cream. I would climb into the large black chair and say, 'short back and sides, please', which was probably just as well as I don't think Mr Harford's repertoire extended much further. Perched on the chair, I would look around and see advertisements for Brylcreem and various men's toiletries for sale including little pale blue packets of Gillette safety razor blades. And perhaps for the men, there was something for the weekend ... but aged 10, this area of life was an unknown, unknown.

For the shopkeepers, trading was an all-consuming way of life. Half-day closing on Wednesday afternoons, Sundays – and Saturday afternoons for some shops such as the butchers – were the only breaks. I doubt there were many holidays taken by the shopkeepers of Higher Bebington and many other small shops up and down the country at the time. Near the Post Office in the row of shops on Teehey Lane was Mr Grant, who owned the electrician's shop. Wearing his brown cotton twill overall, he and his wife were tied to the counter opposite the front door of that shop for several decades. My childhood use of his shop coincided with just one decade in his long career at it. A young Mr Grant had set up business before the war in these premises when the shops were built in 1932 – just before my grandparents' house was built. It was a time when the ownership of radios was booming, although television was still some way in the future and before 1939 could only be watched in the far-off south around London. The shop window display I remember was not the original one but had probably last been changed in the mid-1950s and consisted of two or three life-sized cardboard cut-outs of young women in pleated skirts advertising Ever Ready batteries against a backdrop of vertical strips of faded crepe paper in cream and pink.

The shop interior was stacked solid with old radios and television sets, leaving just a narrow corridor from the shop entrance in a straight line to the counter. It suggested that Mr Grant had lost control of his business many years earlier and that time had left him behind. In 1935, he was probably a 'genius' – a 'whizz' – when it came to repairing valve radios; but possibly the advent of transistor radios after 1960 had left him behind. So, the old radios and TV sets simply piled up. The story is that they were radios that had been brought in for repair but never returned to their owners. Many were old bakelite wireless sets and early televisions with tiny screens, some of a pinkish hue, rather than the green-grey like ours at home. Perhaps it was all this early plastic along with the varnished wood of other sets – off-gassing – in high levels of concentration which gave this shop such a distinctive atmosphere.

I was a regular customer of Mr Grant as a boy of 10 or 11. I bought batteries for my torches, lengths of wire cable and tiny light bulbs, which I attached with plasticine to six-volt batteries in order to light up min- iature room interiors I used to make out of old shoeboxes. I also bought my bicycle tyre puncture repair kits from him. When I returned to Higher Bebington through the 1970s and into the '80s, Mr Grant's shop was still there unchanged: the cardboard ladies – now very faded – and the crepe paper – now bleached and almost colourless – were still there and, inside, so was Mr Grant. I remember calling in on one occasion and asking him if he remembered me, but he did not. I was probably unrecognisable. By then he must have been about 80 and he seemed to be on his own. I guessed his wife had died but he knew of no other life than to put on his overall every morn- ing and open the shop. Latterly, I suspect, he sold virtually nothing, apart from the odd battery. I cannot remember exactly when I last saw his shop as it always was – perhaps about 1990 – and I suspect that Mr Grant carried on, opening for business every day until he breathed his last.

Shopping out of the way, there was always lots to do on a Saturday. If the weather was fine I played in the garden. A favourite pastime was to make bows and arrows, so I could play Robin Hood with John Savage next door, or I rode my bike up and down the road, or played with balls and marbles. If the weather was poor then I had my indoor interests, my hobbies. Chief amongst these for several years was stamp collecting. In 1963 Dad started my collection by giving me some stamps from Nigeria. Like our British stamps, these bore the crowned head of Queen Elizabeth II. I saw nothing unusual in this. In fact, quite the reverse. Many of the stamps I acquired came from the dominions and colonies of the British Empire and they all shared the familiar effigy of the British monarch. At Mill Road School, world maps on the classroom wall showed Canada, large parts of Africa, India and the Far East in red, with Britain – the mother country – naturally placed near the centre. But by the time I began collecting stamps, the British Empire was in rapid retreat. Nigeria had achieved its independence in 1961, as did many other colonies around this time. I was only vaguely aware of this. Mum told me that the Empire was now called the Commonwealth, but this made little difference to me: the Queen was still its head and I was complacent in the knowledge that Britain was still a 'Top Nation'. It seemed natural to me that we regularly came second or first in the Eurovision Song Contest – and that the England Team would lift the World Cup in 1966: that of course was an opportunity for the Post Office to issue a special stamp proclaiming 'England Winners'.

Stamp collecting was easy, affordable and sociable, and I soon became a keen collector. My mother rooted out her stamp collection for me. Dad found me more stamps – he had his own boyhood collection from the 1930s – and one or two other discarded collections came my way. I also built up my collection by swapping stamps with friends at school. Chief amongst these was Christopher Wathan, who lived in a 1930s semi just across the main road in Shawbury Avenue. We used to meet after school and sit cross-legged on the carpet in his parents' front room negotiating the exchange of our duplicate stamps. The Post Office at the Broadway in Higher Bebington sold stamps and stamp hinges in cellophane packets for sixpence or nine-pence, and then there were the new special issues released by the Post Office several times a year. The first special issue stamp I purchased was the 3d in the Red Cross Centenary Congress set in 1963. Stamps commemorating the 400th anniversary of the birth of William Shakespeare appeared the follow-ing year: I purchased the lower value stamps in the set on the day they were issued, 23 April 1964, but my spending money did not stretch to buying the more expensive stamps in the set valued at 1/3 and 2/6. Two rather ugly stamps – in my opinion – were issued in 1965 to mark the life of Winston Churchill: he had died in January that year. Rather more attractive stamps were then issued to mark anniversaries of the Battle of Britain and the Battle of Hastings, and there were also sets featuring wild flowers, British birds and, from 1966, Christmas. Dad grumbled that there were now too many special issues, but he still bought them in blocks of four, which always impressed me but was beyond my limited means.

I collected stamps for several years but tended to flit from one interest to another. In 1964 I discovered plastic Airfix kits. There was a toy shop at the top of Town Lane that, curiously, was run by a rather unfriendly woman in her 50s or 60s; she seemed to dislike children and perhaps, having seen a lot of them, she did. It is most likely that my first ever Airfix kit, which was a diesel shunter, was probably purchased in her shop. Airfix kits were seduc-tive and the assembly invariably started in a mood of optimism with lofty expectations for the finished product. It was exciting, opening the box and then looking at the individual parts and snapping them off the plastic frames they came on. Then there were usually some superb transfers for the livery of the locomotive or aeroplane. Least interesting, perhaps, was the folded sheet of instructions.

This model, of a diesel shunter, had three wheels either side, joined by a coupling rod. I had no idea that the special glue, which came in small tubes, had to be applied sparingly if the wheels were to stand any chance of turning: too much glue and the plastic began to disintegrate. Soon the wheels and coupling rod of this shunter were glued solid. All my early optimism had evaporated, and I abandoned the attempt halfway through. Although it was only a diesel, I was annoyed I had made a hash of it. My next effort was a model of a Supermarine S.6B seaplane, but this was soon another painful memory.

Another early foray into the world of Airfix was tackling a model of Charles I. There was a series of Airfix models of famous historical figures, which included a Julius Caesar and an Oliver Cromwell. I ruined my Charles with the finish. The paint was Humbrol enamel, which came in little tins, miniatures of full-sized paint tins with lids that showed the paint colour. But these were glossy and runny and showed every drip, and besides, ended up everywhere; on my clothes, all over my hands and fingers and thus on everything nearby, which sometimes got me into trouble; only white spirit or turps could clean the mess. Gradually my technique improved, and I turned to aeroplane kits, and built a Fokker Friendship aeroplane in Aer Lingus colours and then a BAC 1-11. Paying more attention to the instructions and using the smallest dots of glue to join the parts, the completed models, painted and bearing their transfers, were just about passable and displayed in my bedroom.

Like most boys of my age and era, I also had a collection of Dinky and Tri-ang die-cast metal toys. They were mainly various types of cars. A favourite was a Triumph Herald in pale blue and white, but my very favourite was a Dinky model of the *Mallard* steam locomotive that came with two red and cream coaches: this was in effect a Dinky car in the shape of a train as the three parts ran on rubber wheels. I used to take them to school, where I would 'race' my cars (and *Mallard*) against other boys' cars in the school yard at 'playtime'. I also had three model Tri-ang ships and a set of Lesney Matchbox 'Models from Yesteryear'. This boxed set included a red vintage bus, a London tram, a steam traction engine, a Morris Cowley bullnose car and, best of all, a lovely model of the *Duke of Connaught*, a late Victorian single-wheeler express engine of the Great Western Railway. I later added to this series with a Rolls-Royce Silver Ghost, a green steam road roller and a blue steam wagon; some of these were presents, of course. The Tri-ang ships and the Lesney vintage vehicles were 'Sunday best' toys that I played with on the window sill in my bedroom – away from the hurly burly of the kitchen floor – and as a result, most of them survive in good condition, having become vintage toys in their own right.

My great childhood regret was never owning an electric train set. I always hoped to have one but the nearest I ever came to this was receiving a Hornby O gauge clockwork train set for Christmas about 1963. The track was a simple circle and the bright green engine whizzed round and round until the clockwork motor wound down – which didn't take long. It seemed a little dated. I soon lost interest and cruelly scrapped the engine and tender, although I still have the sturdy orange-coloured box it came in as I upcycled this to make a miniature cottage interior. The engine was a Number 30. One day I will buy another to make good this wanton act of destruction.

Another interest at home when I was about 8 was the creation of a little garden down the side path of the house. This was a garden in miniature with little paths and borders and a tiny pond made by sinking a jam jar in the soil. I soon replaced this with an old plastic washing up bowl, which I disguised with moss and stones around the edge. I took my pond quite seriously and wrote a brief history of it with diagrams in 1966, recording the state of the water – how I cleaned it – and describing the pondlife it contained (mainly tadpoles).

For an hour and a half on Sunday mornings, the Light Radio made contact with British forces posted overseas in West Germany and further afield with *Two Way Family Favourites*, a record request programme punctuated by the BFPO (British Forces Post Office) numbers, which led me to wonder if the Second World War was actually quite over. At 1.30 p.m. around the time that cooking of the Sunday roast came to a head with terse observations, such as 'it needs another ten minutes' and the making of the gravy, the bandmaster, Billy Cotton, came on the air introducing his show with his memorable cry of '*Wakey, Wakey!*'

Our Sunday lunch took a decided turn for the worse as far as I was concerned around 1963 or 1964. There was nothing more I liked than meat and two veg with gravy – *Ah Bisto!* – And lots of mashed potato. My contribution to the meal, often coinciding with the start of Billy Cotton's show, was to mix some Colman's mustard powder with water in an egg cup.

But in 1962, the *Sunday Times* inaugurated the first 'coloured supplement'. My parents revered this innovation in newspaper publishing. Every issue they kept until there was quite a pile of them in one of the bedroom wardrobes. The *Sunday Times Coloured Supplement* included recipes by Robert Carrier (1923–2006), chef, restaurateur and cookery writer. His was a name that came to fill me with dread as his recipes ushered in a food revolution within 1 Orchard Way. For the time my father had fairly progressive ideas about food, doubtless the legacy of his days in the Merchant Navy. He grew Jerusalem artichokes, shallots and garlic in the light sandy soil of the back garden and used to buy various items such as brown rice and cakes made with dates from the Birkenhead Health Food Shop. So, in 1 Orchard Way, Robert Carrier was kicking on an open door.

The Old Roast Beef of England – garnished with my carefully made mustard – disappeared from the (pale blue Formica) table and in its place arrived goulash and Boeuf bourguignon, chili con carne, minestrone soup and Kareninan luncheon dish. There were new flavours made of bouquet garni, basil and other herbs, and there was lots of garlic. Meat was marinaded for hours on a low heat in red wine, and I was miserable. I didn't like the flavours and found this new style of cooking unappetising – apart from the Kareninan luncheon dish made with minced beef covered with melted cheese and served on rice, which I have to admit was very tasty. But generally, I did not want this foreign food, I wanted spuds and gravy and roast meat with carrots, turnip or sprouts. I sulked and protested – and so did my sister, Janet, but this was a minor food revolution that doubtless touched other homes across Britain in the 1960s. For my parents there was no going back: Robert Carrier was king and my mustard days were over.

This new style of Mediterranean cooking also brought wine – mostly red – to the kitchen table. A small glass was often poured into the sauce gently simmering over the iron hotplate and my parents would drink more of the bottle with our meal. Until then I don't remember much alcohol in the house. On Friday and Saturday evenings, Dad routinely went to his local, the George Hotel, and drank beer by the pint. On Saturday evenings he used to return late, after we were in bed, with a small bottle of Babycham for Mum and very often for us children, a copy of the *War Cry*, the newspaper of the Salvation Army; they doubtless went on dry pub crawls on Saturday nights to collect donations and sell their paper. In the mid-1960s, wine drinking was new and novel. The printed information titled, 'Taking a bottle

Home', at the front of my 1965 Cavendish Diary reflected the general lack of familiarity with wine at this time:

> In this country many men miss a great deal of pleasure and interest by never venturing beyond whisky and beer in their drinking … many people hesitate to buy wines for themselves or their guests because they do not know their way around the complicated lore and ritual of wine-drinking …

I rather doubt that, aged 9 going on 10, I ever read this section of my diary, but the advice continues to reassure the adult reader that only a very few 'wine-rules' really matter. Along with these hints and tips, my Cavendish Diary for 1965 also contains notes on fishing, cricket – and to prevent the denting of the male ego – ordering a restaurant meal. It was very much a man's world and I was glad to be a boy. I remember the first time I tried red wine when I was about 8. Dad poured a small drop into a glass. I sipped it, anticipating it would be sweet and delicious with an intense aroma of blackcurrants – in other words, like Ribena – but to my disappointment, I found it sour and dry. Nevertheless, it was tolerable when diluted and for Sunday dinner I was often given a little wine watered down with tap water.

Occasionally, on Sunday afternoons, once Janet and Helen were a little older, the five of us would go for a walk. It was a short distance from our house to the top of Village Road and Storeton Woods across Mount Road. The woods formed a narrow strip of pine trees, birch and oak on the crest of a sandstone ridge and on the eastern boundary along Mount Road the woods were bounded by a sandstone wall. They were divided by Rest Hill Road, which was, in effect, a continuation of Village Road at the junction with Mount Road. The first time we took this walk was about 1963 and Helen was still in a pushchair. It was a short walk down the first 200 yards or so of Rest Hill Road to the other side of the woods. From here the view opened up spectacularly to reveal a wide expanse of rural Wirral. Immediately before us the road dropped steeply and then zig-zagged around field boundaries and hedgerows in the direction of the small settlement of Little Storeton, which was dominated by a Dutch barn and a cluster of miscellaneous buildings. Beyond Little Storeton there were more fields, and a straight row of tall poplar trees, which marked the route of Lever Causeway: a road that the industrialist William Lever had constructed, linking Storeton Road in Prenton – where I was born – with his home, Thornton Hall.

In the distance could be glimpsed the faint blue-grey outline of the Clwydian range of hills across the River Dee in North Wales. It was an impressive prospect and my first real contact – on foot – with the countryside.

As we reached the western edge of the woods, my father pointed to a short length of railway track – bright and shiny through constant wear from pedestrian traffic – which stuck out of the edge of the road tarmac. He explained that it was from the old Storeton 'railway', which had closed many years ago. I imagined a main line with trains of red coaches but, as I subsequently learned, this was a quarry tramway that took stone from the Storeton quarries by horse and gravity down to the River Mersey. We continued our walk. It must have been a fine day in March or April as there was lesser celandine growing in some of the shallow ditches along the lower stretches of the road. I was taken aback by the absence of pavements, kerbs, gullies and drains – and street lamps. Until now, save for the occasional car or train journey, my existence had been purely suburban. The countryside seemed raw and unpredictable. There was a strong smell of manure in the fields … 'Smell that country air,' said Dad, breathing in deeply as an invisible gas cloud from semi-liquid pig manure wafted over the roadside hedgerow.

Once we had reached the bottom of the hill we came across a pretty, dark red brick cottage with stone-mullioned and diamond-paned windows, standing on its own in an untidy garden on the right. In fact, everything about this dwelling was rough and untidy, so different from the suburbia less than a mile away in Higher Bebington. I can't remember how we met the occupant (a scruffy, smiling old lady with white hair, a whiskery chin and wearing a long black skirt tied around her waist, I think with postman's string) but somehow we did, and my parents purchased half a dozen eggs from her. The attraction, of course, was that these were free range hens at a time when most eggs sold were from battery farms. This became a regular part of the itinerary when we repeated this walk over the next few years and we came to refer to this cottage as the 'Egg House'. The cottage is still there, much smartened up now: it was clearly an estate cottage of some sort and displays the date, 1863, carved in stone on the gable end, but for me it will always be the 'Egg House'.

A little further on we entered Little Storeton – the first 'village' I ever knew first hand, although it is but a small hamlet with no parish church or village Post Office. Perhaps not the prettiest village or hamlet in England but it felt special – quiet, tranquil and refined – and different to the suburbia

I knew. I surprised my dad on one of these walks by spotting that a farm building here contained a blocked up pointed arched window. This structure, I later found, was Storeton Hall, built by William Stanley in *c.* 1360, and had later been converted for agricultural use. Our subsequent walks sometimes took us back home in a circle via Red Hill Road, or the other way along Lever Causeway, and so we returned, slightly footsore, to paved roads of suburban housing. Back to familiar territory.

At home on a Sunday afternoon, at 4 p.m., the radio blared out the theme music of Alan Freeman's *Pick of the Pops* with its countdown to the top ten hits and the Number One. At 6 p.m. the mood changed entirely when *Sing Something Simple* was introduced by Jack Emblow and the Cliff Adams Singers. I found this programme rather depressing, probably because the close harmony singing of the theme tune played on an accordion presaged the end of the weekend and the start of another week of school. The strains of 'Sing Something Simple' are inseparable in my mind from sitting at our kitchen table to a tea of sardines, or tinned salmon or Cheshire cheese accompanied by a salad of lettuce, water cress, spring onions, radish and tomato – and loads of salad cream. My mood was generally solemn and subdued as the light faded on another weekend.

A view of Teehay Lane looking in the Birkenhead direction towards Christ Church. Town Lane falls away to the left. All these buildings, except for the church, have gone. On the left is Kings Farm with Pear Tree Cottage, dating to 1734. It was named after the espaliered pear tree on its south-facing gable. Oil on canvas by Harold Hopps (1879–1967), early 1900s.

Village Road from a postcard used in 1910. Fifty years later the thatched cottage and the gas lamp had gone but otherwise the road was little changed. The spire of Christ Church is visible over the rooftops. My school friend, Michael Ainsworth, lived in the late Victorian house on the extreme right.

Left: oil canvas portrait of Margaret Coucil by Henry Carr, *c.* 1925. Right: Fred Jenkins in 1919 from a postcard.

The Dining Room at 178 Higher Bebington Road, watercolour by Fred Jenkins, October 1946 with an eighteenth-century panelled oak chest and green carpet.

Left: Janet and I in the front garden of 1 Orchard Way, June 1961. Right: Helen aged 2, fletton brickwork and light yellow roughcast, pale blue paintwork and the hammered glass front door.

'Getting Ready for School' from *Today & Tomorrow* edited by E.R. Boyce, 1962 – a composite and idealised scene with the accent on hygiene; nevertheless, a picture of everyday life for a young family in the early 1960s that is illustrative of some aspects of life in 1 Orchard Way at the time. Living is centred on a modern kitchen with a stainless steel sink and an easy to clean pale blue Formica-topped table. Cooking, eating, washing up and getting ready for school all take place in the kitchen.

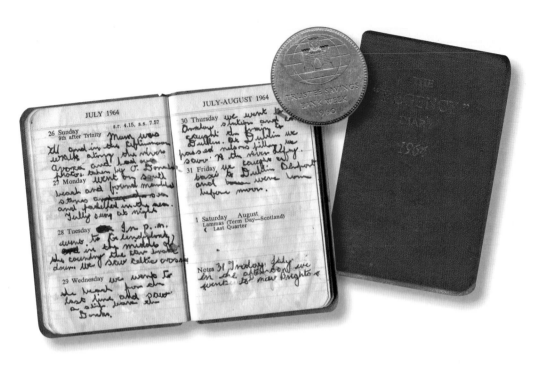

Trustee Savings Bank medal, 1960; my diary for 1964, a present from Barbara James – my 'Auntie Barbara' who lived in Rock Ferry – for Christmas 1963.

A sixteenth-century sea battle drawn at school by me, aged 8, using lead pencil and wax crayons for the colour. The red biro comment came from Mr Boyce, class teacher at Mill Road School in 1964.

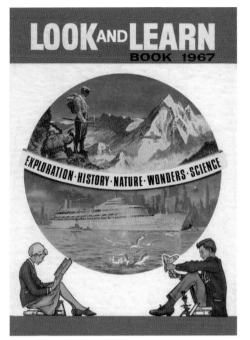

Left: the front cover of the 1967 *Look and Learn Annual*, a Christmas present for 1966. Right: circular jigsaw of famous London scenes by Waddington. A Christmas present about 1964, which for several years shaped my perception of London.

I collected the tea cards contained in packets of Brooke Bond PG Tips tea. Transport Through the Ages was my favourite set, collected in 1966.

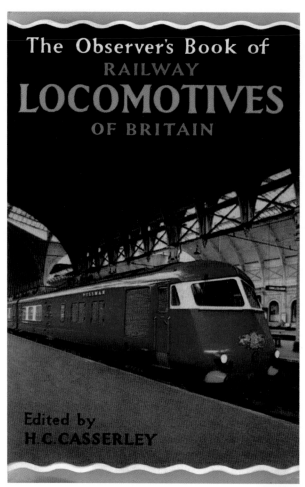

Dustjacket of *The Observer's Book of Railway Locomotives of Britain*. First published in 1955, this is the 1962 edition, which I purchased in February 1964.

Locomotive 42587 by the coaling stage at Birkenhead Shed on the last day of steam passenger trains from Birkenhead and of through trains to London Paddington, Sunday, 5 March 1967. I saw this engine the previous day at Port Sunlight heading a train towards Chester. The main part of the depot is just visible in the background on the left. (C.M. Whitehouse)

A wet day in the 'quaint' streets of Barmouth in July 1963. Wrapped in plastic macs and sou'westers, Barbara Eveleigh is holding Helen. Looking thoughtful and running my fingers along the top of the wet wall, I am wearing a black plastic mac.

The Mini-y-Mor hotel, Barmouth, *c.* 1950s. The walled garden is at the side of the hotel on the right.

Higher Bebington Mill in happier times. The mill is shown from the south with some of its outbuildings, probably about the time it ceased working in *c.* 1901. Its sails and gallery are intact and it appears freshly whitewashed. The field in the foreground is now occupied by late twentieth-century housing.

The track bed of the Storeton Tramway on a slightly raised embankment in the northern half of Storeton woods, now a popular route with dog walkers. Photographed November 2015.

The 'Egg House' built in 1863 on Rest Hill Road, Storeton. Photographed March 2019.

Watercolour I painted of a winter scene with a low red sun, influenced by the walks to Little Storeton, painted at the kitchen table on a Saturday morning *c.* 1964. The rural lane on the left is lined with old-fashioned street lamps.

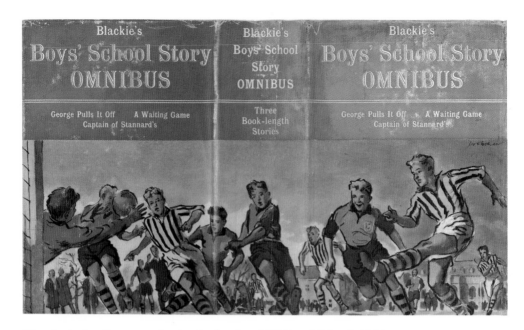

The dustjacket from my school prize book at Mill Road School, 1964.

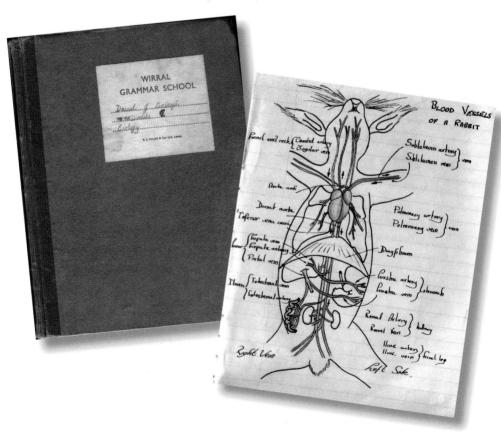

A fourth year biology exercise book and a diagram of the blood vessels of a rabbit.

The badge from my school blazer, *c.* 1969

My enamel school lapel badge.

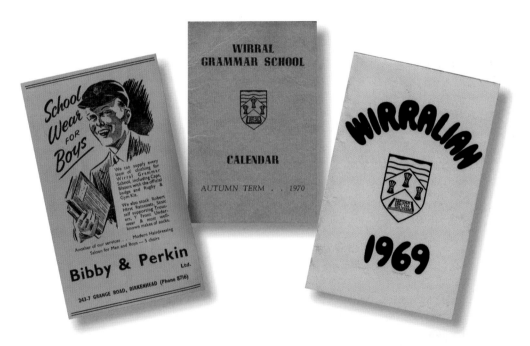

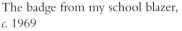

Left: Advertisement from the school magazine, *The Wirralian*, 1967, although by this date virtually no pupils wore the school cap. Middle: Wirral Grammar school calendar for autumn 1970. Right: *Wirralian*, the school magazine for 1969. This issue introduced a new style cover with a 'Flower Power' style font that sat uneasily with the school badge.

The shops on Teehey Lane, *c.* 1970. Grant's electrical repair shop is behind the telephone box; the Co-op supermarket is behind the letter box. The Fina petrol station is just visible on the left. The spire of Christ Church is in the distance and the bus is heading towards Birkenhead.

A Birkenhead Corporation bus ticket, 1960s.

Birkenhead Woodside, *c.* 1969. On the right is one of the Leyland Titans operated by Birkenhead Corporation from the 1950s. Next to it is a single-deck Crossville bus on a Chester service and on the left is 'our' bus, the 64 that ran to New Ferry via Higher Bebington. The Liverpool waterfront with a sooty black Liver Building forms the backdrop.

34 Devonshire Road, Claughton, Birkenhead, drawn by E.R.F. Cole, a lecturer at the Liverpool School of Architecture, for a Christmas card to my grandparents, *c.* 1935. It is the left-hand house of a pair built of Storeton stone probably around 1840.

GREETINGS

FROM ETHEL & EDWARD ·R·F·COLE
34 DEVONSHIRE ROAD·BIRKENHEAD·

On 31 July 1964 we took the ferry from Woodside to New Brighton. Standing on the upper deck my father took this photograph of a Blue Funnel ship, recognising it as one he had served on. The vessel is probably *Calchas*, a Class A ship of 1946, which left Liverpool the next day.

Postcard of Dublin Airport with an Aer Lingus Fokker Friendship that I purchased at the airport in 1964.

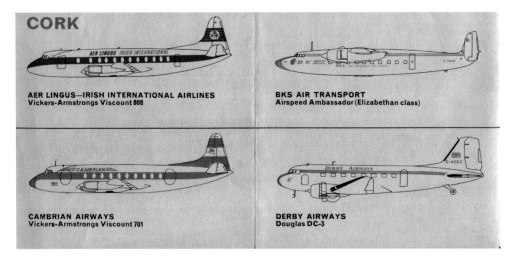

From the Esso Guide to Irish Airports, *c.* 1964. These four aircraft were regulars at Cork Airport and also commonly seen at Liverpool Speke Airport. The Cambrian Airways Viscount that crashed into a factory in Speke on its approach to the airport on 20 July 1965 was of the type depicted here.

A John Hinde postcard of a farmer taking his milk to the local creamery to be pasteurised. The caption adds, 'the patient donkey and cart still hold a position of importance on the Irish Farm', *c.* late 1960s.

Castletownshend from a John Hinde postcard bought for 6*d* in the village post office in late July 1969. The castle is just visible on the right below St Barrahane's Church. Three old stone warehouses line the harbour.

Entrance to the 'Secret Garden', Shana Court, Castletownshend. When this photograph was taken in 1993, the wooden door from the yard into the kitchen garden had gone but the garden was still a semi-wilderness.

Below: Castletownshend. The octagonal tower near the church steps; on the left is the cottage, home to an elderly woman in the late 1960s; photographed in 1993.

8

The Facts of Life

In June 1964, I recorded proudly in my diary that I was top of the class. In this summer, aged just 9, my life changed forever in a way I was unable to control. I fell in love. Most boys of that age had little to do with girls. They played different games, played with different toys – boring ones, like dolls; they sewed or knitted and were, therefore, generally of little interest. Moreover, girls were bossy; they were killjoys, telltales – or simply irritating. To call another boy a 'sissy' was, indeed, a cruel insult. And so boys either tolerated girls, or more usually, ignored them. Of course, it is very likely that aged 9, girls are more mature than boys; and therefore, more sensible, responsible and more likely to achieve at school. And conversely, girls simply tolerated boys … but how could a boy of that age, more intent on playing cowboys and Indians, Robin Hood, riding a bike or fishing for tadpoles, have had the insight to understand that?

Aged about 8 going on 9, one of the very worst of girls in my class was Linda Shorrock. She was noisy, argumentative, loud and bossy. I didn't like her at all. Then something happened. One fine day in spring or early summer, she walked into school in a soft, linty, cotton summer dress. It was a pale, aquamarine blue. I suddenly noticed her dark flashing eyes, her dark – almost black – hair, her slightly tanned legs and arms. She had navy blue or black shoes, which she was wearing without socks. I was stunned. I was transfixed. I was in love. She was – I realised, now – quite simply gorgeous.

Linda was blissfully unaware of this but I wanted her to love me back. I used to shyly pass her little scribbled love notes – her desk was just one in front of mine, so that was easily done. She was never particularly interested in me, although she did once consent to come and look at my little garden plot with its miniature pond. For some two years she was rarely out of my mind.

Even now I can remember her address in Arnot Way, Higher Bebington, and also that her grandfather owned the stamp and coins shop on Borough Road in Birkenhead.

In the background was the popular music played on the Light Radio. I remember the first time I heard a Beatles number on the radio. I was in the garden, just outside the back kitchen door. The number was 'Twist and Shout'. The sound was like nothing else I had ever heard. There was a clear sense – even to an 8-year-old – that something very new and very different had arrived, although I wasn't sure I liked it. This particular number sounded raucous, harsh and aggressive. But soon everybody seemed to be talking of 'Beat Music' and the 'Mersey Beat' was a big part of it.

Suddenly The Beatles were everywhere. They were the 'Fab Four' and everyone, so it seemed, had their favourite Beatle, although for a while I pre-ferred another Mersey Beat group, Gerry and the Pacemakers, then a band name with no possible connections with heart surgery. But everyone was talking of The Beatles. There was even a white sliced loaf called Ringo Rolls.

Class 1, Mill Road School, Summer 1966. David is seated second row, second from the left. Ted Robins is behind his right shoulder, Christopher Wathan is second from the left on the front row. On the back row, Michael Ainsworth is third from the right and Roy Lowry, a keen train spotter, is far right.

A neighbour who was a hospital ward sister proudly told us that she had cared for George Harrison's aunt. My final year class at Mill Road School in 1965 included Ted Robbins, a slightly chubby boy with a dimpled chin and glasses, who told us he was the second cousin of Paul McCartney. His parents ran the small shop on the corner of Village Road and Mount Road opposite the Travellers' Rest pub; it was called The Corner Cupboard.

Ted and I became good friends for a while when we were 10 going on 11. We used to play marbles at his house and several times went fishing together after school in some of the ponds that lay in the fields below Storeton Woods. With a jam jar each we collected frog spawn, tadpoles, water snails and water boatmen and a minnow or two, and I added my catches to my pond. One evening after school, our expedition was delayed as Ted's fishing net had to be repaired by his father before we could set off. By the time we finally made our way through Storeton Woods and across the fields leading to the pond it was probably not far off the time I was expected back home, so when we did finally return to the village, it was to see my mum walking towards us along Mill Road weeping, worried and upset; once home I received a serious telling off for being so late.

Ted and I performed a disastrous double act in the school's summer field games in 1966 competing in the 'wheelbarrow race'. I was the wheelbarrow and Ted the pusher but within a second or so of the start of the race we ended up in a heap and came near last. Once we left Mill Road we drifted into other friendships. Ted is now known to many as a radio and television entertainer and star of *Coronation Street*.

My crush on Linda was probably fading by the time I left Mill Road School in the summer of 1966. I had passed the eleven plus selection and was bound for Wirral Grammar School at the beginning of September. Of course, aged 10 going on 11, loving Linda meant kissing and cuddling. I understood nothing else. Then, so far as sex education was concerned, that summer I suffered a major reversal. My dad decided to tell me the facts of life. We were on holiday in Guernsey. We were in our hotel room. It was early evening. I think my mother was bathing my two sisters. So, my father and I were on our own …

Dad opened the conversation unexpectedly. 'You know when you get an erection,' he said. Replying in a diffident, non-committal sort of way, I replied 'yes', as if to say, well 'maybe … possibly'. I think I wanted the conversation to end, but in a sincere but grave manner he continued.

He explained how the man contained a seed in his testicle. I thought, oh yes, I know about that, believing the entire gland was the seed, and reflecting that passing this almond nut-sized seed over to the woman would bring tears to my eyes. He added, 'Of course, it is very painful for the woman.' I think he might even have mentioned blood. I flinched and created my own picture of sexual intercourse: a solemn (and painful) duty that was undertaken just once, usually on the wedding night. The newly married couple would stand either side of the opened toilet, in their pyjamas, their bare feet on the cold bathroom floor. The man would (painfully) expel the almond-sized seed and then, causing even more pain to his bride, slot it into her via his outstretched hand and fingers, just in case it shot off and slid into the toilet water. The notion that intercourse might take place in a bedroom, might involve a kiss or two and a cuddle – and might even be pleasurable – never entered my head. I started my grammar school education that September with a lot to learn.

Part 3:

1966–69

9

Grammar School

Tuesday, 13 September 1966. Morning. My first day at Wirral Grammar School. I was fully prepared. My parents had received advance notice that I was in Dodds – the red house – and so I arrived for 8.45 a.m. wearing the house tie. I was very pleased about this. I hadn't a clue why the house name was Dodds. Sounded a bit like Ken Dodd. But red was my favourite colour. I was in full school uniform: dark grey socks and black shoes; dark grey short trousers; a white (nylon) shirt – the tie with its red diagonal stripe and a dark blue blazer bearing the school badge on its breast pocket. It was a handsome badge: a heraldic design in silver, gold, white and blue that incorporated the wheatsheaf of Cheshire – and the school motto, *Sapientia Ianua Vitae*, or Wisdom is the Gateway to Life. I also had a school cap, but I think I lost that on Day Two. If not Day Two it had certainly gone by Day Five. I also had a rucksack – or 'haversack'. Army issue. Purchased at the Army and Navy Stores in Birkenhead.

So I was ready. We began the day in the main assembly hall. We were addressed by the headmaster, Bernard H. T. Taylor, a remote and introverted man, bald with spectacles, who always wore a black academic gown. More memorably, those of us who had been selected for Dodds were addressed by the house master, Mr Blackwood, in the same hall. He was also wearing a black gown and similarly bespectacled and bald. There were about twenty-six or twenty-eight of us. We made up the first year of Dodds. We were 1D. And we were told that we were 'the chosen' – the lucky ones – selected (I know not how or why) for Dodds. I was happy, because I was in the red house. The other houses were Barber, coloured white; Hodgson, they were bright emerald green; and Lever, who wore yellow. Blue was the school colour that we all shared. Lever, I knew, of course. He was something to do with Port Sunlight, but it was only many years later that I learned the identities of Dodds, Barber and Hodgson.

I guess that the house masters of the other three houses made similar introductions. We were all lucky. Every new boy was given an identity within the school that was chiefly manifested through achievement on the sports field. This was a state grammar school, established by Cheshire County Council, but the ethos and structure the education committee had created when the school was first established – including the house system and the designation of school prefects – were modelled on the public school. Football was not allowed on the school pitches; that, we were told, was the game of the secondary modern boys. We played rugby. Football was the passion of many of the boys, however. No one I knew actively supported Tranmere Rovers; it was all about Liverpool or Everton, although there were a few Manchester United fans: one boy in my year had the name 'George Best' heavily inked on his haversack. Football was only tolerated at break and lunchtime on the tarmacked yard – for those interested – and played on a sort of 'five-a-side' basis.

Wirral Grammar School for Boys in Cross Lane, with pre-war bungalows on the opposite side of the road. The girls' school is out of view to the left on Heath Road. From a postcard, c 1930s.

Probably within the first hour we took our places in our classroom; ours, I recollect, was Room One: a ground-floor classroom which faced onto a tarmacked inner quadrangle. The assembly hall made one side of this square and the other three sides contained classrooms all accessed by a corridor, open on the inner side to this quadrangle. First-floor classrooms were accessed the same way: by a first-floor balcony reached by steps made of concrete or composite in the corners. This balcony also looked out onto the quadrangle. There were more classrooms on the other side of the assembly hall creating a second quadrangle, although this one was not quite so complete and included several single-storey structures mainly housing the craft workshops, which were later additions. The school, with its impressive neo-Georgian façade fronting Cross Lane, had been designed by the Cheshire County Council architect in the late 1920s. It was very typical of local authority buildings of the inter-war years. There was a near identical school for girls around the corner on Heath Road.

A long-enclosed corridor led from one corner of the first quadrangle to the canteen. Beyond that, the corridor extended to a new four-storey block that had just opened. This contained the library on the ground floor with the upper floors dedicated chiefly to languages, geography and, on the top floor, art. With separate access, the girls' school had use of one floor. At the rear of the main block, there was a wide tarmacked yard – or playground – used at break time and lunch. The end of the yard nearest the new tower block was bounded by a new gym and the other end by a thin copse of trees and two portable buildings that housed the music department. Beyond the yard there was a large sports field divided into several pitches with rugby posts in place. There were several small copses down each side of the field and in the distance on the skyline could be seen the dull red brick tower of the old windmill.

So there we were, Form 1D, taking our seats for the first time at desks in Room One, our base for the next ten months. A few boys I knew from Mill Road School, like Kevin Grundy from the Post Office. But most of the class were strangers – from Lower Bebington, New Ferry and Bromborough – and from further afield: Eastham and Ellesmere Port, places I scarcely knew. My world was widening, and rapidly. And so was my vocabulary. As our class teacher made his introductions, some of the boys on the front row made signals behind his back with their fingers. 'Why are you giving the Churchill Victory Salute?' I asked one of these boys later in the morning when we were taking our break. He and one or two others sniggered slyly at my ignorance. So that's how I was first introduced to the f★★★ word, but I was not likely to become one of their friends. Other 'rude' or swear words circulated the classroom – and came mostly from the lips of these boys, or lads – as we were generally known – who came from New Ferry, Bromborough or Eastham: industrial areas, and they were harsher, rougher and worldlier than I. They used words and phrases new to me, like 'yer wot', 'go'ed' and 'com'ed', spoken with a guttural scouse accent. I soon came to realise that life at my junior school in Higher Bebington had been gentler and more innocent.

Our class teacher was Mr Colburn. He was 'Sir' to us, and we were all addressed by our surnames. So to him, the other teachers and all in my class, I was simply 'Eveleigh'. We sat in rows of desks from front to back in alphabetical order: at the front of the first row nearest the windows was Bailey, followed by Boyd (another boy from my junior school), Buxton and Cassia. This was Stephen Cassia – the very same – who, six or seven years earlier had thrown me backwards off the canteen bench on my first day at school. I was at the back of the second row with Davies, Dempsey and Dragoonis in front of me. At the back of the row nearest the inner wall was Wright, a quiet boy with red hair and freckles, who quickly proved himself the brightest boy of the class. Mr Colburn had his own desk, facing us at the front, and behind him was a blackboard fixed to the wall with a shallow tray at the bottom running its full width for bits of chalk and the wooden-backed 'dusters'. The blackboard itself was very wide, almost the entire width of the front wall. The floor was boarded in deal and the wooden desks were relatively old and unpolished. I recollect that the walls were painted a flat pale green. The result was that the classrooms of the original part of the school were rather sombre and had a distinctly 'woody' smell.

Mr Colburn was an English teacher, an elderly man to us, with thinning, wavy grey hair and glasses – another for whom the academic gown was standard attire; the sleeves and skirts of the gown were used frequently to wipe the blackboard. He was a Lancashire man, from Burnley, with a slight Lancashire accent who always pronounced the words 'plaster' and 'apparatus' with a short 'a'. He could appear slightly absent minded and even tentative – thus he often confused me with a classmate by the name of Havard – but he could also be irritable and a disciplinarian at times. He was definitely 'old school'.

We were all issued with a smart pocket-sized booklet of six pages with a blue cover, bearing the school shield. This contained the programme of

Detail of a photograph of first to third year boys at Wirral Grammar School taken in 1968. From left: Bernard Thornley, History; Gordon Youd, Geography; John Haworth, Head of Chemistry; Oscar Wilson, Deputy Head; Bernard H.T.Taylor, Head Master; George Colquhoun, Head of French; A.N. Phillips, German and Religious Education and far right, D. Jones, Head of Art.

significant dates and sports fixtures for the coming term and also a page laid out as a timetable with squares for the days of the week and the eight 'periods' of each day. Over the next few days, armed with this timetable, we got to know our daily routine and to navigate our way around the school, and so we met our new teachers and subjects new to us, such as Latin, biology and technical drawing.

Some of the teachers had worked at the school since the opening in 1931. Such was the deputy head, Mr Wilson, who was known by his first name, Oscar; another was Mr Phillips, who was known by the nickname Flopsy. He had written the music to the school song, which began with the lines, 'What shall our wish be/We who are waiting …'. On one formal occasion in the assembly hall, we gave the words the 'shepherds wash their socks by night' treatment when he was leading the song on the piano. Outraged and visibly hurt, he stopped playing and stormed out, to the amazement of everyone gathered, teachers and boys alike. He was a sensitive and, doubtless, a decent man, but that was probably why he acquired the name Flopsy.

At the time we took it for granted that some of the older teachers had seen active service during the Second World War without ever knowing the details. Our form master, Mr Colburn, had joined the school in 1948 but – I learned later – had taken part in the D-Day landings. Mr Philips had served in the Intelligence Corps as a captain. A dapper and affable head of modern languages, Mr McMorine, had served in the Royal Artillery and

Former Wirralian, Prime Minister Harold Wilson, with his tobacco pipe outside 10 Downing Street.

seen action in Algeria and Italy before ending the war fighting communist rebels in Greece.

To my knowledge, these teachers never spoke of their war experiences but they did talk of their recollections of the first member of the sixth form and first head boy, the Prime Minister – as he was then – Harold Wilson (1916–95), who was a pupil when the school first opened in 1931. My first history lesson was memorable. We took our seats and, without speaking, our new teacher picked up a piece of white chalk and wrote the word 'independent' on the blackboard with some emphasis – and even a little irritation. All 'e's he said, no 'a's and no 'i's. Spelling was never one of my strong points, but this was an effective lesson within a lesson for it is one word I have never misspelt. The teacher was Mr Thornley, who was also new. He was a tall man, about 30, slim with long drainpipe trousers, dark brown curly hair and spectacles. He occupied the Old Library on the first floor, above one of the quadrangles; there were glazed library cupboards with shelves at the front of the room that were used to store unclaimed lost property, consisting of a random collection of personal possessions, sportswear and the like, including a size eight white plimsoll.

There were some good teachers at the Wirral, but Mr Thornley was one of the very best. It was impossible to drift off in his lessons. He demanded attention, did not brook any nonsense and was engaging for the entire thirty-five minute period. He was another Lancashire man, from Bolton. He would typically end the last lesson of the term with a treat, reading excerpts to us from *1066 and all That* by Sellars and Yateman or the story of *The Lion and Albert* by Mariott Edgar (1880–1951), which he read superbly in a broad Lancashire accent for extra effect:

There's a famous seaside place called Blackpool
That's noted for fresh air and fun
And Mr and Mrs Ramsbottom
Went there with young Albert, their son

And so it continues. Mr Thornley's sense of humour and of timing ran through his lessons, which were complemented by amusing scenarios or references. For example, when we reached 1485 and the Battle of Bosworth Field (which took about three years as we had begun a slow trot through the ages in September 1966). 'So,' said Mr Thornley, 'don't think that at the end of the battle, the soldiers stood around leaning on their swords and pikes and said, "Right Lads, that's the end of the Middle Ages".' I laughed. We probably all laughed. And of course, I remembered this: it was a memorable lesson in historical continuity. Past eras did not end abruptly with a full stop like the end of this paragraph.

Another memorable teacher was Gordon Youd, who took us for geography. He was always Gordon Youd to us – never simply Mr Youd – and one of just a few who had a first name we knew. I remember him as a pugnacious man, of middling stature, but solidly built with a prominent chin who brought to mind the cartoon character Desperate Dan, only Gordon Youd was clean shaven. He was another effective teacher who ensured that the brand new desks, unblemished, golden yellow and varnished, in his immaculate new classroom, GR2, on the left at the end of the first-floor corridor of the new block, never acquired any graffiti or mindless scratches. He would walk up and down the aisles between the rows of the desks and with great deliberation, his chin up and with some pomposity exclaim, 'Now let us say this, boys …' (a pause), 'a contour is a line that joins places of equal height.' And so, lessons continued like this: a series of short and deliberate definitions or pronouncements of facts – all delivered virtually as dictation in small digestible bites that we wrote down and learned, making sure, all the while, that we did not mark those beautiful yellow desks.

I enjoyed geography very nearly as much as history. It was interesting. Especially as we covered the historical geography of our own world, the Wirral peninsula. So, we learned how this piece of land, originally a Saxon 'hundred' in the county of Cheshire and bounded by two rivers, the Dee and the Mersey, had developed according to the variable fortunes of these two rivers. First the Dee had dominated, providing sea passage to Chester, origi-nally a Roman town called Deva. There was even a port on this side of the Wirral, Parkgate. It had silted up long before the 1960s, but I was impressed to learn that George Frederick Handel had sailed for Dublin from Parkgate in 1741 for the first ever performance of *Messiah* the following spring. The Wirral always struck me as something of a backwater where nothing note-worthy had ever happened and no one notable had ever visited – except Ken Dodd, of course, when he opened the Fina petrol station in Higher Bebington in 1964. But to learn that Handel had sailed from Parkgate was – well, surprising.

We then learned how the Dee had gradually silted up, denying Chester access to the sea – and eventually even Parkgate, further down river. And then the River Mersey had become the more important of the two. In con-trast to the Dee, the Mersey had a narrow bottleneck of an entrance between the Wirral and Liverpool that provided a natural scouring of the river course. There was no chance of the Mersey ever silting up. So Liverpool grew. It overtook Chester in commercial importance and then finally, on the banks of the Wirral, Birkenhead with its docks and iron ship building sprang out of nowhere in the early 1800s; Port Sunlight with its soap manufacture and model village followed later in the century; then our maps showed the entrance to the Manchester Ship Canal, which led straight to the heart of industrial Lancashire at Salford. Together they established Merseyside as an industrial region of national significance. The fate of Parkgate, facing Wales with its river frontage high and dry, was to become a favourite Sunday after-noon destination for locals to take a stroll and enjoy an ice cream.

I liked drawing maps of Merseyside in colour in my geography exercise book using my tin of Lakeland colour pencils. Any drawing was enjoyable. Our art teacher was Mr Jones, a small older man with a pronounced nasal voice. There were two art rooms at the top of the new block and art was another favourite subject that always guaranteed me an A grade on my school reports. At the start of one second year lesson, Mr Jones announced that we were going to paint a picture for possible entry in a European day school competition; for our subject we had to select a legend from a European country other than our own. I chose the story of the fourteenth century Swiss hero William Tell and drew the scene where he shoots an apple off the head of his son with a crossbow. I handed in my painting and forgot all about it. Then a few weeks later in the middle of a lesson I was told I had to see the headmaster. Not knowing the reason, I entered his office to be told that I had won first prize in the UK section; an older boy had won second prize in the essay competition and we were photographed together for an article in the *Bebington News*. I received a book token and a bookplate that featured the blue flag of the Council of Europe with its twelve yellow stars. It was the first time I had seen this flag, first introduced in 1955.

With this token, I bought volume one of *A History of Everyday Things in England* by Marjorie and C.H.B. Quenell. This four-volume work for children was first published in 1918; it remained in print for over fifty years. The original aim of its architect author, aided by his artist wife who provided many of the line drawings in the volumes, was to provide a 'picture of bygone times that would complement the teaching of history in schools by describing the surroundings of history'. There were chapters on architecture, transport, costume, country life, kitchens and cooking, and many other aspects of everyday life. For me these books were another starting point of a lifetime's study of the history of everyday life and ordinary everyday things, which, as the authors intended, complemented the history of the school classroom, which closely followed the course of political events.

Unfortunately, as time went on, my school reports developed an asymmetrical profile, with high grades for the arts subjects and indifferent or poor results for some of the subjects on the science side. Biology, I liked. We studied plants and learned about photosynthesis, stamens and pollen. And there was a lot about reproduction; first plants, and then frogs and rabbits. But our learning in this area was confined to the physical facts, nothing behavioural was ever covered; so we drew the reproductive organs of frogs and rabbits in our exercise books without ever addressing the question: why do rabbits 'breed like rabbits'?

I had entered the school with a very incomplete and quite possibly unique slant on the facts of life thanks to my father's tutorial the previous summer.

Needless to say, it was not through biology lessons that the mist cleared but through conversations in huddled, sniggering groups at break and lunchtime, aided by heavily thumbed dictionaries. Before the start of one first year Latin lesson, a boy in the class took some chalk and wrote *amamos nudas puellas* on the blackboard. Mr Moore, the Latin master, was not amused when he entered the room and hastily rubbed it off. Every summer, when we were allowed occasionally on the playing fields at lunchtime, the annual 'charge' of the girls' school took place. Like swarming insects or a herd of randy buffalo, we would charge in the direction of the girls' school. There was never any plan and within a few minutes a couple of sports teachers in tracksuits with whistles brought the nonsense to a close.

If biology was interesting, chemistry got off to a promising start at the beginning of the second year with a spectacular show of pyrotechnics involving potassium, magnesium and potassium dichromate by our teacher, Mr Everett. Unfortunately, none of the lessons after that were anywhere near as exciting as this introduction but chemistry was infinitely preferable to my two least favourite subjects, physics and maths …

Gazing peacefully through the window, my mind wandering, probably thinking about trains – or that other thing we all thought about, apparently something like once every three minutes – I was disturbed from my

Wirral Grammar School, Form 2D, photographed in the quadrangle with the assembly hall in the background, *c.* 1967–68. David is far left on the back row. Richard Wynne Davies is on the front row, fourth from the right.

reverie when, from nowhere, a metre rule struck my desk with a mighty crack. 'What I have just said, Eveleigh?' said a menacing, clear voice. It was Mr Hilditch, the physics teacher. We were in our third year, and this was an afternoon of double physics – yes, that was a whole seventy minutes of physics. His question came completely out of the blue. I had no idea what he had just said. It might have been something about prisms or lenses and the refraction of light, or possibly something relating to electrical circuits. What I did know was that the universe slowed down to almost a dead stop during afternoon double physics. Hilditch stared contemptuously at me. I sat there feeling pretty dumb and stupid and so he set me a punishment: not 100 lines, but 100 physics definitions to be written down and presented the next morning.

So that evening at home, I wrote out Boyle's Law (something complicated about gases) and Newton's Law of Gravity (that apples fall vertically to the ground at a constant speed) and others, and then handed them in the next morning. Fortunately, they were not checked. Through the lessons, Mr Hilditch would typically walk around the room in his academic gown with a tight grip on his metre rule. He was a distinguished-looking man, probably in his mid-40s, with wavy brown hair, greying at the sides, and a piercing stare. His favourite dictum, delivered with sardonic crispness, and occasionally addressed directly to me was, 'simple rules for simple folk'. He was detached and humourless throughout the lessons. I never understood why he had gone metric by 1968. Perhaps the extra 3in of a metre rule produced a louder 'crack' than the 36in of a yard. Certainly, I don't think his rule was ever used to measure anything, it was simply a weapon that looked more scientific than a cane. I do not remember Mr Hilditch with much affection. I think he could have introduced a greater sense of wonder into his teaching of physics, but to be fair to him, I think we would all agree, it is very annoying to be ignored when speaking.

Mathematics was another torture. It was one of those subjects where pupils across all the four houses were placed in four divisions, or sets, according to ability, or recent attainment. I somehow managed to enter the third year in Set Two, which was taught by the music teacher, Michael Hams (another teacher with a known first name). There was a certain amount of mischievous behaviour in his lessons, which I found a welcome distraction, but this was ultimately to my detriment: halfway through the school year, I was demoted to Set Three. My father was furious. He could never understand why I found mathematics difficult, a not uncommon reaction from people who find the subject straightforward. But like physics I found it boring and pointless, as well as difficult. I could not see the purpose of quadrilateral equations, or simultaneous equations; of making x the subject of an equation when it was stuck in the middle of a large and complicated algebraic equation. I quite liked basic geometry and could work out the area of circles and the volume of cylinders but I could never see how knowing that the square of the hypotenuse of a right-angled triangle was equal to the square of the other two sides was ever going to help me in later life. I soon gave up on trigonometry, and any question that had anything to do with acceleration or velocity terrified me as that usually invoked calculus that was completely beyond me. I did not understand the language of maths, of co-ordinates and co-efficients, indices, cosines and cosecs. Looking back, I regret this mental block. I was defeated before I even began.

A much more interesting area of the curriculum was music. I remember our first music lesson vividly. Our teacher was a rather theatrical, grandiose middle-aged man by the name of Mr Hemery. We were offered heavily subsidised lessons (I think there was a small charge each term) to learn a musical instrument. So, in this first lesson, he described the instruments of the orchestra to us, extolling their particular attractions and looking for takers. He began with the strings and one or two hands were raised for the violin. Then he moved to the woodwind instruments. Finally, he reached the brass section: first the French horn, then the trumpet. For the trumpet, a fair-haired boy called Davies put up his hand. 'And now,' he said, 'that magnificent instrument, the trombone. This needs a tall, strapping lad,' he said. 'Someone with a BIG chest and LOTS of puff.' He looked around the class, smiling, waiting for takers. There were none. Then I shyly raised my arm. I was hardly tall and my chest was tiny; in fact, at the time, I was wearing St Michael's white cotton vests for 9-year-olds – much to my embarrassment in the school changing rooms – and I was conscious that not only was I the smallest boy in my class, I was the smallest across the entire first year. I was, therefore, in 1966, the smallest boy in the entire school.

But I fancied having a go at the trombone. It was all down to watching a television showing of the 1954 film *The Glen Miller Story*, just a week or so earlier towards the end of the summer holidays. Miller was the American bandmaster who played the trombone and with 'Pennsylvania 6-5000' and his arrangement of the 'St Louis Blues March' ringing in my ears it had to be the trombone, even if the instrument was nearly as tall as me. Shortly afterwards I had my first lesson with the brass teacher, a trombonist with the Liverpool Philharmonic Orchestra. The school trombone was a slim silver-plated 'pea shooter' with a narrow bell but was soon replaced by a Boosey and Hawkes brass trombone in a large black case, which made a rounder sound. The first thing I learned was how to hold a trombone to make sure the slide would not slide off and hit the floor. Then I learned the positions of the slide as it is extended outwards, although the seventh position when the slide is fully extended was almost beyond my reach. And then, with the aid of the tutorial *A Tune a Day*, I learned simple studies and simple tunes in the bass clef.

Many boys gave up their extra lessons after a few weeks but several of us persevered; one was Davies with the trumpet. After a while, he and I joined the school orchestra. The brass section always sat at the back and the music we played had been scored for schools' use so all the instruments of the orchestra could be involved. Well, some of the time. One of the tedious and sometimes tricky aspects of playing the trombone in any orchestra is counting the bars rest. Very often I would lose count – or simply wander off – so I would miss my cue. The violins, I used to think, had it easy. They usually had the melody, played almost continuously, and so did not have to count empty bars – and they played in packs, so if one made a mistake, I used to think, who would notice? But a mistake by the trombonist – and I was the orchestra's sole trombonist – must have been the musical equivalent of 'blowing a raspberry'. So, our conductor, the music teacher, Michael Hams, would rattle his stick irritably (orchestra conductors are invariably irritable types) on the top of his music stand and I would be singled out to play my part again until I had got it right. Very often, even if the notes were right (and played in the right order), the brass section was frequently criticised for playing too loud and robustly but that was the result of our frustration: after sitting quietly and counting sometimes as many as sixty-four bars rest, when we had our chance, we wanted to 'give it some welly'.

Through the school orchestra I got to know such famous trombone classics as Handel's *Water Music* (we played 'Bourrée', 'Hornpipe' and 'Air') and 'St Anthony Chorale' from Haydn's *Divertimento*, where I played the same part as the bassoon. For the next year or so, until I purchased my own second-hand trombone, the school instrument was my pet. I used to take it home, wash it out and polish it. I used to make myself very unpopular at home with my practising going through my arpeggios and scales and lip exercises designed to strengthen my embouchure. Over time, I developed a good tone, but truth be told, my reading of music was always a bit shaky.

At lunchtime there was a clear split between the sporty types who turned the tarmacked playground into a danger area with balls fizzing through the air and the rest of us who hung around the perimeter for safety, which included the music rooms by the trees over on the left. Sometimes a fight would erupt on the playground to the chant of 'fight, fight, fight' and I once got dragged around the tarmac roughly by my ankles, leaving me with bleeding hands. So the playground or yard could be a dangerous and threatening environment. But it would be wrong to think the musical types were all well-behaved little innocents. My trombone playing got me into serious trouble on two occasions …

The first occurred in my first year. It was a lunchtime and I was due to have my trombone lesson in the music room reserved for practice, but our Latin teacher, Mr Moore, was in the room playing the piano, a baby grand. He did this routinely, which I and others used to find frustrating as it put an end to our own practising and general larking about in the music room, safe from the balls flying about like random cannon shot just a few yards away. So there was Mr Moore, in a reverie of his own, playing the piano when I barged in and said, with excessive glee, 'Sorry Sir, you've got to go now, I've got my trombone lesson.' Now the advantage was with me. He had to go. My lesson was official. And my tutor from the Liverpool 'Phil' had arrived. Without saying a word, Mr Moore got up, closed the piano and left. My lesson went ahead, and I thought no more about it, overlooking the fact that the first afternoon period after lunch on this day of the week was timetabled for Latin.

So, at about 2 p.m., we assembled in our classroom for afternoon Latin, as usual making a lot of noise at our desks. Then Mr Moore entered the room. As was customary, we rose from our seats and the noise fell away to a shuffling silence. Mr Moore spoke, not to the class, but directly to me.

'Come here Eveleigh', he said. Not knowing why, I walked to the front. 'Now bend over,' he said and, using a size eight white plimsoll – or pump as we called them – he gave me 'six of the best'.

As I returned to my desk, rubbing my behind, I said indignantly, 'What was that for, Sir?'

He replied, 'For impertinence.'

For several weeks this size eight pump had been kicking around the room and, on several occasions, had been used as an impromptu instrument of punishment. After my beating, I decided this had to end. So, I took the pump upstairs to the Old Library and handed it in to Mr Thornley as 'lost property'. And this is why the collection of lost property on display in the Old Library included a size eight white plimsoll.

The second brush with school rules involving my trombone took place in the third year when some of us in 3D had acquired the bad habit of missing morning assembly. Curiously, the 1944 Education Act had stipulated that the school day in state schools should start with an act of worship of a non-denominational character, but the assembly usually took the form of a diluted form of the Church of England service. As a result, the Roman Catholic boys were excused and would hang around in the classrooms while it took place. As a Protestant, I should have been present, but I was quite excited that I had just been sent in the post some manuscript music to the theme tune of a TV programme on BBC1 called *Zocco* – an innovative and quirky magazine programme for children that was broadcast on Saturday mornings from 1968. The theme music was a jazzy little piece written and arranged by Brain Fahey (1919–2007), a well-known composer, arranger and conductor for the BBC. I liked it and so had written to the BBC asking for the music. A week or so later I received a reply: I was sent a small sheet of manuscript music with the trombone part, a compliment slip from Brian Fahey and a postcard of Zocco, the flashing, talking pinball machine that presented the programme. So I decided to show off and play the piece to the small group in the classroom who had absented themselves from assembly. My timing, apparently, was immaculate. One or two who were present at assembly later told me that just as the headmaster, Mr Taylor, said with routine solemnity, 'Let us Pray', the jazzy riff of *Zocco* started up in the background. Our classroom that year was Room Six, which was close to the hall. Too close. There was no mistaking my identity: there was only one trombone player known to the school and straight after assembly I was given a detention by our form master.

A detention was a painless but ignominious punishment that involved staying after school – on a Tuesday, I recollect – for an hour and writing lines or an essay. The ignominious part was that the names of all those put in detention were read out to the school in assembly once a week by the headmaster. This happened to me on four occasions in my time at the Wirral but the offences I and others committed were often very trivial; for example, one detention was handed to me because I turned up late for my sitting in the canteen for

The BBC *Zocco* postcard sent to David from composer and arranger Brian Fahey in 1969.

school dinner. Of course, very often the roll-call of boys receiving a detention were the same ones – regular miscreants – and very often notorious ruffians and dunces. Frequently they would notch up more than one detention in the same week. These boys had their names read out in a separate list and we all knew that in addition to the detention they would also receive a caning from Oscar Wilson, the deputy head. If any boy managed to receive three detentions within a week – and that was quite a distinction – he was caned by the head-master. Apart from that I do not recollect much use of the cane at the school and, unlike Mill Road Junior School, no teachers brought a cane into the class, although there were occasions when teachers would smack a boy on the head, and Gordon Youd – and one or two others – were not beyond a little ear pulling and twisting to get a boy who had earned their displeasure to stand up.

Two of the detentions I received were handed out by school prefects. The prefects were distinguished by their blue braided blazers; they also wore an enamel lapel badge bearing the school shield with 'prefect' in an arc across the top. So a prefect was easy to spot. One prefect detention was handed out to me for hiding with a classmate under the teacher's desk during morning break to avoid been thrown out into the freezing cold. The second was for calling a prefect a rude name. Teasing and baiting school prefects was one of the norms of school life and one morning, aged about 12, Davies and I ran after a prefect called Larter and shouted out that he was a 'farter'. Well, perhaps this was not an accurate description of this upper sixth former – and was not that funny either – but I think we were both surprised to find our-selves in detention the following week.

Other miscellaneous recollections of everyday life at Wirral Grammar School are of school dinners – I loved the puddings consisting of pink blanc-mange and large sugary biscuits – and going back to the dinner ladies and, like Oliver Twist, asking for more; of smelly changing rooms, freezing cold and foggy afternoons on the sports fields, bored stiff and numb with cold as I hung around the rugby posts doing my best to avoid being dented by a rugby boot and covered in mud. One winter's afternoon during rugby, in bitterly cold weather, I slipped on a puddle of muddy water that lay over a sheet of ice. I got up with my red Dodds jersey and my white shorts covered in icy cold wet mud. I must have looked pathetic. Mercifully the games teacher sent me back in, or sent me off, for an early hot shower. Another unpleasant memory is of the horrible sickly smell of stale cigarette smoke mixed with that of stale urine in the outside toilet block – we called them the 'bogs' – where some boys illicitly smoked. Being caught for smoking behind or in the bogs was a serious offence but it was legal, of course, in the teachers' staff room. I occasionally had to knock on the staff room door during break time with a message for a teacher and was invariably met by a thick fog of tobacco smoke when the door opened.

I remember my first day in a pair of long trousers. Along with several boys I wore short trousers through the entire first year but shortly after the start of the second year, 'went into longs'. I remember wearing them for the first time and looking down with surprise as the wind billowed up my trouser legs on a draughty autumn morning in one of the open corridors. I remember the school library, reading all the Biggles books and the adventures of Sherlock Holmes, – that is when I wasn't reading books on local history, the history of railways, or looking up information about trams, traction engines and windmills in the sets of encyclopedias.

There were school trips too. In the first year, in November 1966, we went to Chester by train with Mr Thornley and Mr Moore, our Latin master. I enjoyed walking around the near complete city walls but the displays of Roman coins and tombstones with their Latin inscriptions in the Grosvenor Museum did not interest me; ancient history at the time held little appeal, for I could make no connection between my environment and life 2,000 years ago. Later in the first year, in April 1967, I made my first trip to London with the school's railway society. The novelty was the journey from Liverpool to London on one of the new 100mph electric trains in their smart new livery of blue and pearl grey. Travelling across London mainly by tube, we visited two railway sheds: Finsbury Park near Kings Cross and Old Oak Common west of Paddington, which by then were both 100 per cent dieselised. We ended the day at the Clapham Transport Museum, where I saw rows of brightly painted Victorian and Edwardian locomotives, trams and the streamlined *Mallard*, the fastest steam locomotive in the world; I had noted with relief several years earlier in 1964 that the preservation of this locomotive in a museum was secured. I bought an enamel lapel badge of a locomotive (the *Evening Star*) and then we returned to Euston. Before boarding our return train, I hurriedly bought a coffee in a thin plastic beaker from a kiosk and scalded my mouth drinking it, a hard-learnt lesson for life. Most of the return journey was in the dark and we arrived at Liverpool Lime Street about 10 p.m. I was met by my dad, who was incredulous that we had toured around the capital without seeing a single one of its famous sights!

The rail ticket for the school railway society trip to London, 5 April 1967, along with a souvenir ticket from the Clapham Transport Museum and a lapel badge of the locomotive, Evening Star, both purchased the same day.

A few months later, on Saturday, 1 July, Mr Thornley took me along with two other boys – Wynne Davies and Keith Doyle, who was a year or two older – in his pale blue Morris 1100 to the tramway museum at Crich in Derbyshire. It was a sunny day and we explored the site located in a former quarry. We had rides on two beautifully restored double-deck Glasgow trams; one had open balconies front and back on the upper deck, the other was fully enclosed. But many of the trams we saw that day were in a hopelessly derelict condition. I remember there was a lot of shattered glass on the ground from the broken windows of unrestored trams. The museum venture was then still relatively new and a lot of restoration work lay ahead. I bought the museum catalogue and overnight became a dedicated tram enthusiast, searching wherever I could for information about trams and making coloured drawings of them. The attraction, of course, was that trams ran on track like railway trains, but I felt there was something poignant about the decline and closure of Britain's tramways. Nevertheless, I was surprised to find that a handful of urban tramway systems had struggled on within my lifetime: Liverpool only gave up on its trams in 1957, Sheffield in 1960 and Glasgow in 1962, leaving just the famous seaside trams of Blackpool. So I felt sad for their demise but glad that a handful had been rescued and returned to working order.

Formal school visits included geography field trips to North Yorkshire, and in March 1968 we headed by coach to North Yorkshire to see the White Scar Caves and Thornton Force waterfall near Ingleton. This provided my first ever experience of motorway travel. My last ever sighting of a steam locomotive on British Railways occurred on the return journey from this trip: a type of engine, known to us train spotters as a 'Stanier Black Five', was travelling light on the main line beside the M6 between Preston and Lancaster. The following year we headed to Malham in Wharfedale. Starting with Janet's Foss waterfall, we walked over to Gardale Scar and climbed up the left-hand side of the waterfall to Malham Tarn and then continued to the sheer cliff face of Malham Cove, learning all the while about the erosion of carboniferous limestone by streams and acidic rain water.

I also look back fondly to friendships, above all with Davies. As we became friends we dropped the surnames. His first name is Richard but at school he was known by his middle name, Wynne. Sometimes rivals and briefly enemies, friendship was ultimately the stronger force as shared interests and outlooks drew us together. When we were about 12, Wynne and I used to meet up at the bottom of his road, Princes Boulevard – a leafy road of '30s semis with wide grass verges – and walk into Lower Tranmere to Byrne Avenue Baths for a swim. On the walk back, famished, we would stop at a fish and chip shop and spend 9d on a fried potato scallop and chips.

We also shared an interest in coin collecting. Around 1968, aware that pounds, shillings and pence were soon to be phased out and replaced with a new decimal coinage, we were infected by a craze of the time for checking small change for old or rare coins. Articles in the press highlighted the fact that all silver coins dated 1946 or earlier were 50 per cent silver and that any silver coin minted before 1920 was 0.92 sterling silver, and therefore worth more than its face value. Armed with a little pocket book called *Check Your Change*, which gave values for each coin according to its date, rarity and condition, Wynne and I used to comb through the small change of the boys in our class, especially on Monday mornings when we arrived at school ready to hand over 5s of weekly dinner money to our form master. In theory all silver coins from 1816 were still legal tender in the late 1960s and all 'copper' (actually bronze) coins from 1860. I never found any silver coins earlier than 1920 in anyone's change, but old and worn black pennies and halfpennies from Victoria's reign were not uncommon, especially those of the late 1890s and up to 1901 that bore a bust of the old Queen wearing a lace veil as in the iconic Jubilee portraits. But one morning around 1968, as I was about to leave for school, I spotted that one of the three pennies Mum had just given me for my bus fare was an older and scarcer bun-head penny, which depicted the Queen as a younger woman. It was worn almost flat and the Queen's bust was but a ghost of the original design, but the date was still decipherable: 1860 – the earliest possible date for a penny in circulation. I had never come across one this old. Incredibly this coin had seen at least 108 years of life and was still in daily use as legal tender. When it was minted the Queen was only 41, Prince Albert was still alive and Charles Dickens had just begun the serialisation of *Great Expectations*; Lord Palmerston was Prime Minister and the American Civil Wars were yet to start. Needless to say, this coin was not passed over to a bus conductor that morning but joined my growing collection. It was yet another way in which we caught the tail end of Victorian life in our everyday lives in the 1960s.

Wynne and I also gravitated towards Christ Church, the parish church on Kings Road, where we got involved in serving as altar boys and bell ringing. There was a rota arranged for the bell ringing organised by Brian Savage, one of the two boys next door, and then eventually an older boy from school, Michael Blackburn. We rang the bells on Sundays, for Holy Communion at 10 a.m. and Evensong at 6.30 p.m., and occasionally on Saturdays for weddings. There was fierce competition to get on the weddings rota as we were paid a guinea in cash in the form of a green pound note and a shilling by the verger, Harold Hamer: to us this seemed like a small fortune. Like all vergers of that time Mr Hamer, as he was known to us boys, went about his daily business in a black cassock, except when he was employed grave digging.

Ringing the bells was a solitary experience as they were operated single handed using a simple wooden device called a carillon. On the uppermost floor of the tower, level with the pairs of louvred arched windows, there were eight bells, each resembling a giant bicycle bell, which were fixed vertically in a horizontal row to a timber frame. The bells remained stationary: it was the clanger that moved, operated against a counterweight by steel cables that connected to the wooden carillon two storeys below. The eight bells formed a major octave and so the carillon had eight wooden handles, rather like the handles of an old-fashioned wooden wheelbarrow arranged in a row at roughly waist height. These were numbered one to eight and each was connected to a cable: depressing the handle rang the bell. The carillon enabled us to play both simple peals and hymns by numbers; the hymn, 'Holy, Holy, Holy', for example, began with 88 66 444.

In 1968, the church tower was then not 100 years old – it had been added to the original church in 1885 but to me it felt like the tower of an ancient castle: it smelled like any old church – slightly damp and musty – and had a stone spiral staircase to the ringing chamber over the porch and small lancet windows with thick leaded panes. The first time I explored the tower I was very impressed to find a large old Bible in this chamber. It dated from the 1850s and at the time was the oldest book I had ever seen. Ringing the bells for Evensong on a winter's evening by the light of a naked 60w pendant light bulb was a spooky experience. It was always my plan to secretly enter the tower when it was Wynne's turn, so I could scare the living daylights out of him by making ghostly moans from the floor above, but I never got around to it; once, however, I did manage to trap him in the crypt but immediately felt ashamed of myself and let him free.

My four years and a month at Wirral Grammar School was a time of mixed emotions, highs and lows, triumphs and a few disasters – or at least embarrassments. A microcosm of life and a taste of what lay ahead in adult life. I made some good friends and still have the copy of *The Observer's Book of Music* signed by ten members of the Young Musicians Society and presented to me when we left the Wirral to start a new life in Amersham in Buckinghamshire; one signature is 'R. W. Davies (Friend)' and over fifty years on he still is. Looking back, I was privileged to be educated at a state grammar school with dedicated teachers. But it could have all have been so different.

Firstly, for me: I was fortunate to pass the eleven plus. There were a small number in my class at Mill Road Junior School who failed the selection and were 'condemned' to a secondary education at New Chester Road Secondary Modern. I can remember their distress the morning the announcements were made. My year, 1966, was the first to be tested by continuous assessment, which probably – and hopefully – provided a more accurate method of assessment than a one-off examination. I was just so profoundly grateful that I had 'made the grade' and was going to the Wirral. I used to reflect that had I been subjected to the trauma and stress of the eleven plus examination I might have flunked it and ended up at New Chester Road, a prospect that terrified me, for at Mill Road children spoke of its roughs and toughs, though I doubt they were any worse than those that made it to the Wirral! So, I was lucky and fortunate to experience the grammar school regime, however archaic some of its practices might seem today.

Secondly, the school was fortunate. It survived. In the late 1960s, in response to the historic circular 10/65, issued in October 1965 by the then new Secretary of State for Education, Tony Crossland, which introduced the principle of comprehensive education for the nation's schools, the option adopted for Bebington was to create a comprehensive co-educational system for 11- to 18-year olds. When the plans were published in 1968, they outlined the amalgamation of the two grammar schools – the boys and the girls – into a huge mixed-sex comprehensive school. I was only marginally aware of the political undercurrents at the time but certainly thought that the days of the school as a grammar school were numbered. It did strike me as ironic that Harold Wilson, of whom some of the teachers were so proud (and who was a loyal and committed Old Boy of the school), led a government that was committed to the closure of grammar schools, and therefore the demise of his old school. But his government was committed to social equality: the idea that one size fits all was in the ascendancy. However, education is one of the most kicked about of political footballs and when the Conservatives formed a new government in the summer of 1970, the new education minister, Margaret Thatcher, issued a new circular that allowed each authority to decide its own policy. So, Wirral Grammar School survived and has since modernised and adapted to new methods of learning and new educational models and structures that have enabled it to preserve its identity as a grammar school. Just as I left the school in September 1970, I knocked on the office door and bought an enamelled school badge. It was the same as the prefect badge, only without the title, and was available to fifth formers and above. It cost me 5s. Now the badge is some fifty years old and a precious tangible memento of my time at the school.

10

'Progress'

Friday, 14 March 1969. It was cold, cloudy and grey, a typical March day. Early evening BBC1 Children's Hour was shared by *Crackerjack* and *Junior Points of View* presented by Robert Robinson. *Thunderbirds* was on the 'other side'. The Plaza in Birkenhead was showing *The Good, the Bad and the Ugly* starring Clint Eastwood, but I had something else on my mind. A terrible event was underway near the top of the village. The old windmill was coming down. There had been talk of this for some time but now it was happening. The owner, Alun McDonald, a local builder and developer, had sought and been granted permission to demolish the mill to make way for new housing. The demolition was carried out using a wrecking ball suspended from the jib of one of two cranes brought to the site. The operation had started the previous day with the removal of the brake wheel from the top of the tower. By Saturday afternoon the mill was down; all that remained was a pile of rubble, broken timbers and dust. It was like a public execution. I stood in stunned silence – holding my bike, one of a small crowd – with tears in my eyes. The site was relatively open, so choosing a moment, I rooted out part of a cast iron cog wheel and some fragments of timber, put them in my bicycle satchel and rode home.

At that moment I hated Alun McDonald with all the hate I could muster. How could he do this to such a wonderful building that literally towered over Higher Bebington village and bestowed it with character and identity? How many places had their own mill? But we let ours go. The following week the demolition was featured in the *Bebington News* with the headline, 'The Old Mill Bites the Dust'. The article explained that permission was granted following a survey by the borough engineer and surveyor, T.H. McGrath. There were, indeed, some horrible cracks in the brickwork,

Now over fifty years old, yellowed and faded, David's newspaper cutting from the *Bebington News*, 21 March 1969, featuring the demolition of Higher Bebington Mill the previous week.

but the mill stood firm – apparently – on sandstone. And probably would have continued to stand firm, I guess. So perhaps it could have been saved, but this was the 1960s. There was then a mindset that nothing should stand in the way of progress. Progress! A word and an outlook that banished debate and swept aside any idea that things from the past might enrich our lives.

I was not quite 14 but for me the issue, put simply, was about what looked right. I remember on one of our train journeys to Yorkshire a few years earlier, probably around 1963 or 1964, seeing the first high-rise office blocks going up in Manchester as our train approached Manchester Exchange. The new blocks, to me, seemed to strike a jarring note. They were out of proportion with the old townscape around them: they were too high and too dominant. But it was not fundamentally about scale. After all, many older buildings on prominent city centre sites were large and worked well. One I knew well as a child was the Liver Building, which loomed sooty and black over the Liverpool water-front, then not far away there was the red sandstone Anglican Cathedral – at the time still under construction; there were also many Victorian and early twentieth-century public and commercial buildings in both Liverpool and Birkenhead, not forgetting the Victorian railway termini.

The key is that these buildings were designed within the same architectural lexicon and with the same traditional building materials – natural ones, like stone and local bricks – that had been used for centuries. The Liver Building, completed in 1911, was of course, inspired by the early high-rise structures of Chicago and was one of the first buildings of reinforced concrete built in Britain, but it was clad in granite and the scale of its detail and the language of the exterior design – from the rusticated ground floor to the clock towers – was familiar and complemented its two neighbours, the Cunard Building and the Mersey Docks and Harbour Board Offices built around the same time. But the slabs and towers that went up in the 1960s were made of untreated concrete with uninteresting facades that largely consisted of repetitive rows of windows. This was the Brutalist style of architecture that, arguably, brutalised its surroundings, but took its name from the French *beton brut*, meaning raw concrete.

I was quickly made aware that not everyone saw things as I did. A day or two after the windmill's destruction, I tried to share my sorrow with the police sergeant, Dave Mitchell, who lived in the bungalow opposite. 'Well it was a bit of an eyesore,' he replied. So not everyone mourned the passing of the mill, nor probably the other old buildings that had disappeared since the 1950s in Higher Bebington. Of course, the fundamental flaw in the logic of my position – that is, a wish to see old and historic buildings conserved or at least readapted for modern use – is that, unchallenged, we might all be living and working in wattle and daub or stone huts, all of them listed by Historic England. Progress is inevitable and without it we would have no heritage to preserve.

The fact remains that some pretty awful planning decisions were made in the 1960s in towns and cities across Britain. One of the most infamous and still deeply regretted by many was the demolition in 1962 of the massive stone Doric Arch of 1837 at the entrance to Euston station. As a boy railway enthusiast, I knew of this; Mr Savage, our neighbour, had sent me a postcard around 1964 of the grandiose interior of the Great Hall as it had looked in the 1830s. In Aylesbury, just to take one town I came to know later in my teens, an entire historic thoroughfare, Silver Street, was virtually swept away in a major reworking of the town centre in the mid-1960s to create new county council offices, a new bus station and shopping precinct, all in grey concrete; bits and pieces rescued from Sliver Street were saved for the collections of the County Museum. It was the same in Bristol. First it was the fifteen-storey Robinson Block by Bristol Bridge, which in 1963 replaced a handsome Victorian structure, albeit damaged in the Blitz. By 1970, much of the old city centre had been swamped by an invasion of concrete and glass office blocks, drowning out the towers and spires of medieval churches. Only the intervention of John Betjeman in 1971 saved the city from the construction of a large modern hotel block next to Brunel's Clifton Suspension Bridge spanning the Avon Gorge. There are similar horror stories of destruction – and of a few near misses – for almost every town and city across Britain.

I had been fascinated with Higher Bebington windmill for several years before its demolition. In my last year at Mill Road Junior School, I recollect that we 'did' a project on the windmills of the Wirral. In addition to the well-known and preserved mill standing on Bidston Hill, there was a mill converted to a house at Willaston and a derelict sandstone tower, partially clad in ivy, at Gayton, near Heswall. But by the 1960s most had gone. In the early 1900s, one of the last millers of Willaston windmill, Wirral's tallest, recollected that it had once been possible from his mill to see the sails of mills at Burton, Gayton, Irby, Bidston, Bromborough, Eastham, Higher Bebington, Neston and Saughall all in motion on a windy day. At Wirral Grammar School I looked up information on windmills in the two encyclopedias in the library – *Encyclopedia Britannica* and *Chambers* – I think the latter had the best cutaway drawings of the interiors of the three major types of windmill: post, smock and tower. The surviving mills of Wirral were tower mills. Gayton was the oldest and built of sandstone but Higher Bebington Mill and the other were brick tower mills of several storeys and all dated to the early 1800s. They were impressive structures, regularly whitewashed and most built with a timber gallery running around the outside wall. I was very keen to get inside our mill and several times after school cycled the short journey to see if I could find a way in, but in the face of tall steel gates, 6 or 7ft high and armed with barbed wire, my resolve failed me. But I used to stare up at the silent brick tower with its dark empty windows and wonder how the machinery was arranged, how many gear wheels there were (I used to call them cog wheels) and on which floor the millstones were situated. The mill was not just a building, but– like a longcase clock – a working mechanism; that was part of the fascination.

According to an elderly resident, Elizabeth Chamberlain, interviewed for the article in the *Bebington News*, the mill was always whitewashed every two years on Whit Monday. She had lived in Mill Terrace, a late Victorian red brick terrace, behind the mill for about seventy-six years. She remembered the last miller, Harry Johnson, who died in 1947, and also that the flour was taken away in horse-drawn wagons by the miller's own horses, which were stabled in the mill yard. An interesting detail she recounted was that the old sail cloths were prized by local washerwomen as aprons. As a young girl, Mrs Chamberlain will have witnessed the closure of the mill – about 1901 – its gradual deterioration including the removal of the sails during the First World War – and then the destruction of the cap in a storm just after my grandparents moved to Bebington. And then finally, she saw its demolition on those overcast days in mid-March 1969, very likely standing somewhere near me.

So Higher Bebington lost its windmill. Ten years earlier the last quarry to operate in Higher Bebington had closed and when I was about 12 or 13, in 1967 and 1968, exploring the derelict quarries either side of Mount Road became another weekend pastime. On summer Saturday afternoons I explored Storeton Woods on the far side of Mount Road, often accompanied by a school friend, Michael Ainsworth, who lived in a Victorian house on Village Road, near the George Hotel. Initially the attraction was simply that these were woods: exciting and unpredictable, full of steep hillocks and hollows, an adventure playground for exploring, racing up and down the hummocky paths and playing hide and seek. But gradually I came to understand that some of the hollows and sandy outcrops, partially covered in oak, birch and pine, related to the old quarry workings and the route of the long closed Storeton Tramway, which I had first learned about on those Sunday afternoon family walks when I was about 8.

The hard white sandstone had been quarried on Storeton Ridge for centuries. It had been used for several important buildings in Liverpool and Birkenhead. Clambering through the woods, we worked out the rough location of the quarries in the northernmost part of the woods. This was the terminus of the tramway, where a large depression marked the site of the northern quarry. After leaving the quarry face, the tramway had swung sharply to the left and south, running on a low embankment just inside the western edge of the woods. This is clearly seen today and is a popular footpath through the woods. On the western edge of the trees, the line had crossed Rest Hill Road, which divides the woods into north and southern halves. It was here that a piece of track was still visible several years after my dad had first pointed

The tramway tunnel in the southern half of Storeton Woods with the track in place, but appearing overgrown and disused, from a postcard used in March 1904.

Part of a length of fish-bellied Storeton Tramway rail with a cast-iron chair visible on the left, excavated by David and an old school friend, Keith Doyle, in September 1975 near the site of the demolished crossing keeper's cottage in the northern half of the woods.

it out to me around 1963. It was partially embedded in the tarmac of the road and stuck out at one end, pointing the way forward into the southern half of the woods. Here the tramway continued in a straight line, still running parallel to the edge of the woods but now occupying a shallow cutting that had originally deepened as the line curved to the left and east and passed in a tunnel under Mount Road [see map on page 29]. Old photographs show an impressive deep cutting with sheer sandstone walls leading to the roughly cut tunnel portal, but by the time I tried to make out the course in 1967 this major feature had all but disappeared as it had been filled in during the early 1930s with spoil from the excavation of the Mersey road tunnel. Nevertheless, we were sure that we had located the top of the tunnel opening in a vertical face of sandstone visible below the stone wall that bordered the entire eastern edge of the woods along Mount Road.

Back home I drew several maps of the woods indicating the route of the line and drawing the cuttings and embankments as we had learned at school in our study of ordnance survey maps. I still have a fragment of one of these maps from 1967. This was first-hand field work (albeit not carried out in a particularly scientific way) as there was then little published on the railway, but teachers at the Wirral (such as my English teacher, Mr Colburn, and Mr Hodgkinson, the head of history) told me more about the tramway and how, after leaving the woods, it had passed through the grounds of the school before crossing the road, named Cross Lane doubtless because of the tramway crossing, and on through Lower Bebington and Port Sunlight to terminate at a wharf on the River Mersey.

Mr Colburn apparently had a piece of the original railway track in his garage at home on Teehey Lane. This might have been retrieved from the school playing fields – some was apparently found there – but increasingly in the late 1960s and into the early '70s, I found that as we searched for evidence of the tramway, we were increasingly outnumbered by 'grown-ups' who came along by car. They parked their Hillmans, Austin 1100s and other vehicles by the Rest Hill Road crossing and, armed with spades, shovels and picks, dug out the short lengths of the rusty 'fish-bellied' iron track from the sandy soil and undergrowth, loaded it into the back of their cars and drove off.

This was a period when there was a rapidly growing interest in collecting railway relics and this track had greater significance than its use on a little-known horse-drawn tramway: it was reputedly purchased second hand from the Liverpool and Manchester Railway engineered by George Stephenson when the tramway was constructed in 1837–38. So there was the possibility that famous steam locomotives such as the *Rocket* had passed over these rails some ten years earlier on the other side of the Mersey. With just a push bike there was not much I could do about carrying away a length of track, but we did uncover some in the northern half of the woods, near the crossing at Rest Hill, and I managed to extract one of the iron chairs that supported the track. I took this rusty lump of cast iron home in my bicycle satchel and for the rest of our time in Bebington it was a feature in my little garden.

Locally, Storeton Woods were known to most people quite simply as woods, not as the location of old – and quite possibly ancient – stone quarries. When people spoke of the 'quarry' they meant the quarry at the top of the village – on the near side of Mount Road: my mother had talked of it before I ever saw it. And once I was about 11 I began to roam more freely from home and some of my explorations took me in this direction. The windmill was still there then, of course, and just beyond it – at the end of School Lane on the right, a short and narrow footpath led to the quarry. This was the Higher Bebington White Freestone Quarry that extracted the same hard creamy white Keuper sandstone that had been excavated in Storeton Woods and used for the construction of several public buildings in Liverpool, including the Custom House of 1828, Birkenhead Town Hall and our parish church in Higher Bebington, consecrated in 1859. The quarry was more widely known for yielding fossilised prints of a large pre-historic reptile, the Cheirotherium: I remember there were copies of the prints at Mill Road School and in the porch of Christ Church; there was another in Victoria Hall in the village.

The quarry had finally closed around 1959. Surviving records at Wirral Archives indicate the boiler of the steam crane was last inspected in December 1958, but within a decade the land around the quarry edge had become a wilderness of brambles and gorse. I remember the first time I looked over the edge; it was a breathtaking sight. I looked down into a vast and huge void, like a canyon, with near bare sandstone cliffs that dropped down some 100ft to the quarry bottom, where there was a pool of water. I was astonished to look down on a fully grown tree, probably a sycamore, below me. It seemed incredible that hidden away from the village, yet so close to my mundane suburban world, was this man-made abyss on such a different scale. Looking back, it also seems quite incredible that it was not effectively fenced off to keep children and others away from the precipitous edge. Some children did descend to the bottom, but I never had the courage to attempt this and confined my explorations to the northern and western edge, nearest School Lane. I soon discovered railway track that I think was standard gauge with wooden sleepers in the undergrowth. I was very excited about this and initially thought that I had discovered a section of the Storeton Tramway but quickly realised that it was in the wrong place and was clearly a length of track that had been laid for a travelling crane on the quarry edge.

Teetering on the northern edge of the quarry, I also discovered a very antiquated and rusty steam engine with a tall chimney and other complicated parts. I had no idea what it was. It appeared to be a stationary engine of some sort, but it looked very ancient – like George Stevenson's *Locomotion*

Higher Bebington Freestone Quarry photographed in 1912. The view gives some idea of the scale of operations. The mill had closed over ten years earlier but still retains its sails. By the 1960s the quarry edge was thick with undergrowth.

This steam powered stone cutting engine photographed on the quarry edge on 22 March 1953 is very probably the one seen by David fourteen years later. Storeton Woods are in the background.

of 1825, I thought. I was keen that this engine should be preserved but, at 12 years of age, I lacked the wherewithal to make this happen. I asked an older boy at school to make enquiries, but he also doubtless had no means of saving it; he simply gave me some baloney that he had been told over the phone that it would need new boiler tubes – and other things – which would make the restoration prohibitively expensive. It was probably a stationary steam engine used for stone cutting, and the surviving records show that there was such an engine at the quarry with a boiler fitted in 1937 that had come off a traction engine made by Fosters of Lincoln in 1918. I guess that when the quarry was eventually filled in, this engine was tipped over the edge into the quarry as it was so precariously close to the edge; if so, it will now never be found.

On other Saturday afternoons in 1966 and 1967 I used to catch a bus down to Lower Bebington. I would never admit that my real purpose was train spotting and generally mooching around the railway lines in Port Sunlight. I would airily tell my mum I was going to Mayor Library, Bebington's principal library, to read. I think I went to the library once, maybe twice. On one of these occasions, a cold, dreary Saturday afternoon in February 1967, I went covertly in the opposite direction by bus to Birkenhead railway sheds with a fellow train spotter from school called Roy Lowry. He was an old hand at this sort of thing, a self-confident, seasoned train spotter, and when we arrived at the depot, he knocked on the office door and casually asked if we could look around the sheds. From inside an irritable voice with a Scouse accent gave an emphatic, 'No!' So Roy carried on, followed by me, tripping over railway track, and trembling like a leaf in case we were caught. I had visions of us ending up in a police cell in Birkenhead: that would take some explaining back home, I thought.

So we were in. And over the next hour, I wrote down the numbers of some fifty steam locomotives, some already clearly withdrawn and waiting to be hauled away to be scrapped, others simmering and leaking wisps of steam between duties. As we walked up and down the rows of locomotives under cover in the sheds, I am ashamed to admit that I pinched a lubrication cork from the coupling rod of a large freight locomotive (its number, incidentally, was 92026). I still have that cork. Back in the open, I jumped out of my skin when another large black locomotive (92203) standing in front of us suddenly exploded steam from its safety valves with a deafening roar. I was relieved when we left but exhilarated, too. When I arrived home, my mother noticed that I left oily footprints on the back door mat and I received a telling off. As I took off my shoes by the door, I mumbled something about an oily pool outside the library …

That was my first trip to Birkenhead without my parents. Mum always said that Birkenhead was a dump, and that it was rough. Compared to Higher Bebington, I guess it was both, but gradually by the time I was about 12 or 13 and started making my own journeys to Birkenhead, I grew to see that, even if it was a dump, it was quite a fascinating one. Of course, Birkenhead was overshadowed by Liverpool, which could be seen from many places near our home. From my back bedroom window, I had an impressive panoramic

Locomotive 42942 under the coal stage at Birkenhead Sheds in June 1966. This engine was seen lying out of use in the shed on David's visit. An appeal to preserve the engine made through the local press was unsuccessful and it was towed away for scrapping at Great Bridge, Staffordshire in the summer of 1967.

view of the city; stretching from the centre and the Anglican Cathedral with its red sandstone tower over to the right, it was possible to follow aircraft as they came in to land at Speke Airport. From 1967, the modernistic round tower of the new concrete Roman Catholic Cathedral was added to the panorama and then in 1969, St John's Beacon – a tall concrete tower like the Post Office Tower in London. Liverpool was not simply the regional 'capital' of Merseyside but a major commercial and cultural centre – and a transatlantic port.

Occasionally, as a family we went shopping in Liverpool. The journey, starting from home, took us through Birkenhead. The journey began by catching a bus, either a 60 or a 64, to Birkenhead Woodside. When I was older I always went upstairs with the smokers, so I could look ahead and see more. The buses were always double-deckers – and wore the handsome blue and cream livery of Birkenhead Corporation with gold lettering and interiors of smart dark blue leather seats and chromium hand rails. Like the famous red London Routemasters and many buses of the 1960s, our bus had an open platform at the back. The driver was partitioned off from his passengers by a thick glass screen, whilst tickets were issued by a conductor who walked through the bus with his ticket machine hung from his neck printing pale yellow paper tickets.

The bus followed the main road towards Birkenhead. After about a mile a road sign on the left announced that we had crossed into Birkenhead and we were now in Borough Road, but the same suburbia I knew so well consisting mostly of 1930s semis continued. After passing Prenton Park on the left, the home of Tranmere Rovers with its sheds and towering floodlights, the route took on a busier, 'towny' feel. The pebble-dashed semis gave way to short rows of late Victorian and Edwardian terraced houses with two-storey bays and faced in a hard and garish, bright red brick, probably manufactured in Ruabon in North Wales. Many of the fronts of these houses were embellished with decorative panels and raised bands of terracotta decoration. It was now more interesting. On the left we passed the large modern block of Birkenhead Technical College: my father was on the lecturing staff there for several years in the early 1960s. Next on the left was the Plaza Cinema, which advertised weekly bingo: cinemas, I was aware, were in sharp decline due to the resounding success of television. Bingo gave them a new lease of life, or at least postponed their closure.

As the road approached the centre of the town, the terraced rows were built of a darker, more porous and sootier red-brown brick, probably dating to the construction of Borough Road from the late 1860s. We also passed small shops in twos or threes or in short rows: one I always looked out for was Shorrock's stamp and coin shop, which was on the right. Also to our right was Birkenhead Central Library, an imposing building of white Portland stone set in its own grounds. As our bus reached the centre of the town, it went over a busy junction at Charing Cross. There was, I knew, another Charing Cross in London but it seemed quite appropriate to me that a busy town like Birkenhead should also have one.

This gradual transition from twentieth-century suburban semis to older Victorian and earlier properties is typical of many English towns and cities as main arterial roads find their way to the centre. This same progression, back in time, can be seen elsewhere: in Oxford, Worcester and on several approaches into Birmingham, for example. Typically, other buildings

A rainy day in Borough Road in 1971, shortly before demolition of the Victorian terraced housing lining the road up to Charing Cross, seen behind the Crossville bus; many of the houses are already boarded up. Stepping over dirty black puddles in broken pavements is an indelible memory of 1960s Birkenhead.

punctuate the streetscape: the odd late Victorian or Edwardian pub, an art deco cinema, perhaps, miscellaneous small shops, a Victorian church with a tower and spire – Anglican, usually – or the odd non-conformist chapel; and then there might be a Victorian Board School of the 1880s with large white-painted windows and walls of bright red brick.

For shopping in Birkenhead we would usually leave the bus at Charing Cross. From here it was but a short walk to the principal shops in Grange Road, but if Liverpool was our destination, we continued our bus journey. A little further on, in Argyle Street, looking down on the left I could see a railway line in a brick cutting emerging from a tunnel under the road that apparently headed off to the docks. A tall sooty Victorian brick building had been built in the sharp angle between the street and the railway cutting. The railway track has now gone but this building survives. Next was the Argyle Theatre, built in 1868. I became fascinated, when I was a little older, by the theatre's elaborate Victorian façade and as the bus passed by, I would straighten in my seat and stare hard at the ornate brickwork around the arched windows. The theatre had been bombed during the Blitz, but the façade had escaped unscathed.

There were other signs of bomb damage from the Second World War: occasional gaps in the street that served as ad hoc car parks and these, I was always told, were former bomb sites; I recall there was one in Argyle Street to the side of the ABC Cinema. A few yards further on, the imposing smoke-blackened stone houses of Hamilton Square and the Town Hall came into view on our right. Birkenhead was largely Victorian but the development of Hamilton Square had begun in the 1820s. I understood that these large houses were Georgian in style. My mother told me the original aim was to create a fully planned town of squares and crescents within a gridiron of streets and Hamilton Square at its centre. But the ambitious plans soon broke down with the construction of railway lines, like the one that led off to the docks at a jaunty angle to the surrounding streets. And then there were slum dwellings, tenements, gas works, railway sidings, ironworks and a shipyard, the famous Cammell Laird's. So it was a dump, Mum said, and rough. But I was fascinated by this largely unspoilt Victorian town. Unlike Higher Bebington, where '60s suburbia had taken a strong hold, Birkenhead was full of character and atmosphere.

On other occasions I caught glimpses of other parts of the town. Some journeys home from Birkenhead on the 60 bus route took us up Whetstone Lane, where I saw large early Victorian villas of white stucco with slate roofs near the top of the road before the bus swung sharply round to the right, providing a brief glimpse downhill to the left of smaller terraced houses, the gas works and the railway depot packed with steam locomotives. At other times there were walks into Lower Tranmere along roads of large, dignified Victorian houses. Our dentist, Mr Davies, practised from such a house in Dacre Hill in Rock Ferry, a district of Birkenhead facing the river that had grown from the 1830s with a mixture of fashionable housing, at Rock Park, and then later in the century densely packed rows of small working-class terraced housing in streets near the railway line. As the name suggests, Rock Ferry once had its own ferry service across the Mersey to Liverpool and this operated until 1939.

I used to walk to the dentist with Mum. The house had a large solid front door and inside the entrance on the tiled floor stood an old long case clock: its slow and sonorous tick echoed through the hallway, giving it a certain gravitas. Most of the larger Victorian houses in Birkenhead, as in other

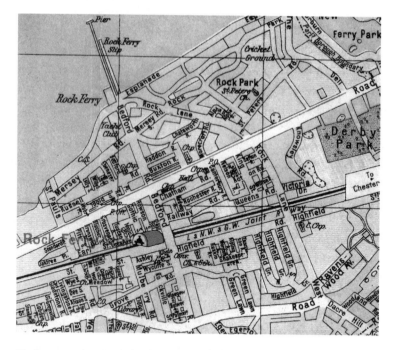

Shakespeare Avenue is lower centre of this detail of a map of
Birkenhead of *c.* 1910; it is one of several streets named after poets
and writers off Highfield Road built about 1900. Dacre Hill is
bottom right.

Highfield Road, Rock Ferry; the houses in nearby Shakespeare Avenue
were very similar.

towns, were set back from the road, offering greater privacy behind solid walls and ornamental gate pillars of blackened sandstone or brick. A mile or so away was Oxton and this was one part of Birkenhead that was spared my mother's general execration of the town. It had expanded from a small village to become an extensive Victorian middle-class suburb with a few grand terraces and many more large detached or semi-detached Victorian villas set in leafy streets. She spoke of it affectionately and told me how as a child she used to accompany her parents when they visited a friend, Eddie Cole, a lecturer at the Liverpool School of Architecture whom Fred had met about 1912 when they were students. He and his wife, Ethel, lived in a substantial early Victorian house of Storeton stone in Devonshire Road with their dog, a black spaniel, Waggy.

Around 1964, one of my mother's friends, Barbara James, our 'Auntie Barbara', who worked for Unilever, took us three children on a Saturday afternoon to Bidston Hill where I saw the windmill there for the first time. Afterwards we went to her house for tea. She lived at 32 Shakespeare Avenue near the railway station in Rock Ferry with her grandmother, 'Nan', Catherine Connolly, a frail, old woman of over 90. This was a very different world from my 1960s suburbia and I felt we had taken a step back in time into Victorian Birkenhead. The house was situated in a small secluded gridiron of side streets with old-fashioned street lamps painted green – not modern-style concrete ones as in Orchard Way. The roads were made up of late Victorian red brick terraced houses, each with a solid wood panelled door, projecting bays and long sash windows in arched openings. We met Nan, who was in the back room sitting in a large comfortable chair watching television. She had been born in October 1873 and I am sure she was the oldest-born individual I ever met (she died aged 96 in 1968): Gladstone was Prime Minister when she was born, and it fascinated me as a boy to reflect that she lived through more than a quarter of the nineteenth century. She will have known a world without motor vehicles until she was an adult, seen fashionably dressed men wearing frock coats and top hats and women in long silk dresses with tight waists and bustles. Working men, roughly dressed in open shirts and waistcoats, smoking clay tobacco pipes … and working women in long aprons and woollen shawls, some balancing baskets and sacks of goods on their heads. Slum children scampering along wet, dirty pavements in bare feet will also have been an everyday sight. Most people, even some of the street urchins, wore a hat of some description. When Catherine

The Mersey Ferry as Catherine Connolly (1873-1968) would have seen it as a girl. From the *Illustrated London News*, 1886. The scene depicts the landing stage at Pier Head, Liverpool with a ferry boat taking passengers for Birkenhead Woodside on the opposite shore.

was a girl there were horse trams on some of Birkenhead's principal streets and she was 4 years old when Birkenhead Woodside station opened, replacing an earlier terminus. The streets were gas lit and roads laid with granite sets. Letter boxes were ornate, hexagonal or fluted, and painted dark green. Letters were still posted with the line engraved 'penny red' stamp introduced in 1841. And there she was, eighty or ninety years after her own childhood, watching early Saturday evening TV, cars parked in the street, and talking to three children from such a different world.

A train journey into Birkenhead passed another part of Rock Ferry at roof level and I remember looking out of the carriage window on a scene that I thought was quite wonderful. There were rows of densely packed Victorian terraced housing with scores of brick stacks and chimney pots above the old slate roofs. Television aerials were fixed to virtually every chimney. It was very similar to the famous scene we saw on television of the roofs of northern terraced housing featured with the theme music to *Coronation Street* on ITV. At the time I believed these houses were very old, simply because they were Victorian, and yet when I first saw them in the 1960s many were probably no older than the average 1930s semi today.

I was also fascinated as a child by Birkenhead Market. It had been built in 1845 by Fox Henderson and Co., the famous engineers who five years later built the Crystal Palace to house the Great Exhibition of 1851. Located near the entrance to the Mersey Tunnel in the town centre, I remember many visits there with my dad on a Saturday morning; it was a brisk five-or ten-minute walk from the main shopping centre in Grange Road. The market was an imposing structure, long and rectangular with tall brick walls, glazed roofs and round arched windows. As we entered the gloomy interior, I thought it looked every bit a railway terminus and was always a little disappointed that it was filled with stalls of fish, fruit and vegetables and not trains.

There are other impressive milestones in the making of Victorian Birkenhead. In my first year at Wirral Grammar School, I was impressed to learn that thanks to an American entrepreneur, George Francis Train (1829–1904), Birkenhead was the first town in Britain to have trams. Then there was Birkenhead Park, the first publicly funded park in Britain, opened in 1847 and designed by Joseph Paxton (1803–65), who also conceived the idea of the palace of iron and glass for the Great Exhibition. I knew there was a Birkenhead Park railway station but never visited the park as a child and it was only many years later that I learned that the inspiration for Central Park in New York came from Birkenhead. Central Park was designed by an American farmer and landscape gardener, Frederick Law Olmstead (1822–1903). He visited Birkenhead in 1850 and was flabbergasted by the new park. 'Five minutes of admiration,' he wrote, 'and I was ready to admit that in democratic America, there was nothing to be thought of as comparable with this people's garden.' Olmstead was impressed that the park could be enjoyed 'equally by all classes', although few people of any class going about their everyday business in Birkenhead in the 1960s probably had any idea that their town had once been at the forefront of innovation and that the world-famous Central Park in New York was based on their own local park.

Back to our bus journey. Just beyond Hamilton Square the bus stopped at the station of the same name. This dated from about 1886 when the Mersey Railway, which joined Birkenhead to Liverpool by a tunnel under the Mersey, was opened. It was another ornate red brick building with an impressive Italianate-style tower that contained the hydraulic equipment that operated the lift down to the subterranean platforms. Sometimes we left the bus here to catch an underground train to Liverpool Central – but if we stayed on the bus a few moments later, Birkenhead Woodside came into view: ferry, railway and bus terminus.

The ferry terminal was directly in front of us and Woodside station, the northernmost terminus for trains from London Paddington, was on the right but the view was dominated by the rows of blue and cream Birkenhead buses parked in straight lines parallel to the station. The buses displayed destinations such as New Ferry, Oxton and Claughton – and a place intriguingly called Noctorum. I vaguely imagined it was always dark in Noctorum and that under a black, starry sky there was some sort of large outdoor aquarium. There was the odd Wallasey bus to be seen in a pale yellow and cream livery displaying seaside destinations such as New Brighton, and then, standing nearest the high retaining wall of the railway station, there were a few buses in a sombre green livery operated by Crosville that mostly went to quiet rural places in Wirral, although a few crossed into North Wales.

On a day of sunshine and slate grey skies, Birkenhead Woodside is recorded looking over to Liverpool in 1954. The station is out of view on the right. The view is dominated by rows of Birkenhead Corporation buses and the liner, MV Reina del Pacifico. The Liver Building was not cleaned until the 1970s.

At the ferry terminal, we bought our tickets at the wooden kiosks, painted light green and cream, passed through the heavy iron turnstile, which rotated with a loud clang, and walked down the covered gangway to the landing stage. As a child I am not sure that I was fully aware that this was a floating stage off land, but I do remember looking with horrid fascination at the oily, dark brown, choppy river water around us. Dad told me it was very polluted and if you fell in the water it would be pitch black. I also imagined it was very deep. I would shudder. We could usually see our ferry boat begin its journey from the Liverpool side at Pier Head near the black and sooty bulk of the Liver Building and as it approached Woodside we could make out the boat more clearly. Although I did not know it, these boats were just a few years old, diesel-powered vessels made in Dartmouth, Devon, in 1959. Some were named after places I knew: one was *Woodchurch* and another, *Mountwood*, named after an exclusive development of early twentieth-century housing between Prenton and Higher Bebington. But as a child, Mountwood was simply part of our 'alpha-numeric' telephone number that consisted of the name of the local exchange combined with a four-digit number. Looking out from the landing stage at Woodside, we watched as the boat approached and as it closed in on the landing stage, we would see a crew member throw a rope over to the stage; once secured, the ramp was lowered, passengers disembarked and then we were allowed on.

We always made our way to the top deck and, looking up and down the river and across to Liverpool, felt the bracing, breezy air in our faces. In 1965, the Mersey Beat in the form of the film and title song 'Ferry Across the Mersey' by Gerry and the Pacemakers, brought this part of my life to national radio and television. I was never very keen on the song. Compared to the group's upbeat hits of the previous year, I thought it was just a little dreary, and I was bemused and almost embarrassed that something as commonplace as the Mersey Ferry was the subject of a pop song. It didn't seem right. But when Gerry Marsden wrote his song, the River Mersey bustled with a variety of shipping. So, whatever I thought of the song, the nationwide attention it brought to the river was well deserved.

I remember one occasion around 1967 or 1968 when I saw a magnificent liner, *The Empress of Canada*, moored near Pier Head in its livery of all-over white with a yellow funnel, the epitome of stylishness. This was a transatlantic liner of Canadian Pacific Steamships and bound for Montreal. At the time I took it for granted that to cross the Atlantic people had a choice of either air or sea travel. In the 1960s there were just a few airlines, such as BOAC or Pan American, flying from a handful of British airports, London Heathrow or Manchester, for example, to North America. Ships such as the *Empress of Canada* and the others I knew of as a boy, such as the Cunard liners, the *Queen Mary* and the *Queen Elizabeth*, looked like 'proper' ships built to take passengers from A to B; they were not the floating blocks of holiday flats that today cruise around the Med and the Caribbean. Apart from the odd liner there were numerous cargo ships, many with red and black funnels, I recall, but it was the ships of the Blue Funnel Line with their distinctive blue and black funnels that always caught my attention: occasionally my father would see one he had served on.

A few years earlier, on 31 July 1964 we had arrived back home before noon from a holiday in Ireland. My parents were not in the mood for unpacking, so leaving the cases in the hall, we made one of these journeys by bus – very likely on the 64 – from the main road in Higher Bebington to Birkenhead Woodside to catch the ferry to New Brighton. Once we boarded the boat, we made our way as usual, to the top deck. It was a warm and sunny early afternoon. Standing on the upper deck, we saw a Blue Funnel ship in front of us. Dad immediately exclaimed that it was one he had worked on; he took a photograph of it with his Kodak Brownie Automatic and told me how all Blue Funnel ships were named after figures from Greek mythology. This one was probably the *Calchas*, which left Liverpool the next day. Other Blue Funnel ships he sailed on included *Agamemnon, Bellerophon, Nestor* and *Telemachus*.

Then we used to see oil tankers with the Shell logo on their short funnels, tugs and dredgers and the ferry boats. Besides the crossing from Woodside it was also possible to reach Pier Head from Seacombe, a little down river past the entrance to the Docks, or from New Brighton. As well as the usual ferry boats we would often see the *Royal Iris*, which looked rather distinguished, I thought, with its light green hull and cream uppers. The *Royal Iris* was a Wallasey ferry boat that was also used for cruises: it contained, so I was told, a dance floor and a bar. As a child I took this busy river scene for granted and thought it was timeless. But like so many railways routes, it was doomed. Passenger and freight shipping was in free-fall decline. Little did I realise that the *Empress of Canada* was Liverpool's last transatlantic liner. She made her last voyage from Liverpool in 1971, a year after we left Merseyside. When I returned to Liverpool in the 1970s, I was struck by how still and empty the Mersey seemed compared with the previous decade.

Left: St John's Church, Grange Road, Birkenhead, 1845-47 designed by Charles Reed (later Charles Verelst). At 150ft this was the tallest church tower and spire in Birkenhead. Right: under demolition in November 1976.

Progress had created Birkenhead. It was a nineteenth-century boom town, busy and progressive, but in the late 1960s and into the following decade a new wave of progress was to undo much of the Victorian achievement. The result was a town that was pulled apart, diminished in character, with the town centre losing its architectural and visual cohesion. As in many other towns, progress was driven by the demands of motor vehicles: ever increasing numbers of cars on the roads rendered Victorian streets inadequate in width and layout to cope with 1960s volumes of traffic. In Birkenhead the approach to the Mersey Tunnel became a notorious bottleneck with jams and delays. The solution was to build a new road system including a flyover near Birkenhead Central Station to improve the flow. The works were inaugurated in 1967 by Barbara Castle, the Transport Minister, and completed in 1969. The flyover had the depressing effect of dwarfing the imposing monument and clock dedicated to King Edward VII that stood on an island of grass close to Central station. Built of concrete, this flyover also looked out of place and out of scale against all the old smoky brickwork of the town. Around the same time, mass destruction of the old terraces lining Borough Road began in preparation for turning it into a wide dual carriageway. By 1969, a fine early Victorian red sandstone church with a slender spire, St John's, located between the shops on Grange Road and Borough Road was left stranded in a wasteland used temporarily as a car park. The church also was ultimately demolished, and the site is now covered by a shopping precinct.

Back home, sitting at the pale blue Formica table, I used to do my home-work, or some of it, and draw and paint in watercolours and pore over my pocket train spotting books published by Ian Allan. The radio would be on in the background. In 1967 the Light Radio and the Home Service were rebranded as BBC Radios 2 and 4. The third (which I was not actually aware of at the time) became Radio Three but most of the pop music we listened to on the Light Radio moved over to the new Radio 1 with its trendy jingles and fast-talking disc-jockeys such as Tony Blackburn, Kenny Everett and Simon Dee. The music was changing, too. By 1967 the pop music of Gerry and the Pacemakers, Freddy and the Dreamers and The Dave Clark Five of just two or three years earlier seemed very dated. But The Beatles were still flourishing and etched into my memory of looking through the glossy pages of my Ian Allan 'ABC' loco spotting books is The Beatles song 'Eleanor Rigby'.

For some young people – that is, older teenagers and young adults – the summer of 1967 was the Summer of Love – of flower power, long-haired hippies, a new type of rock music with lots of fast distorted electric guitar – plus the odd sitar. Pink Floyd, Sgt Pepper's Lonely Hearts Club Band, Procol Harum. Bob Dylan. Protest. Peace Demonstrations. The musical *Hair*. Nudity. And (allegedly) drugs such as LSD and marijuana fuelling psyche-delic art and loads of free sex. This was cutting edge popular culture in 1967. But I saw little of it first hand and had virtually no contact with hippies, psychedelic art and music, apart from what I saw on television. I remember once or twice seeing young men in Liverpool fashionably dressed in old red braided military tunics as if they had just walked out of the Sgt Pepper album cover, or a boutique in London's Carnaby Street, which I always associated with this particular fashion craze. A few older boys at school grew their hair over their ears. There was a sense that such boys were rebels and the Summer of Love, in all its manifestations, was a rebellion, a challenge to conventional ways of living and thinking. Some of those who remember, and perhaps participated actively in the Summer of Love, look back and talk of the optimism and excitement they felt at the time for the emergence of a new, better world. Little of this touched me personally at the time: I thought it was all a bit weird and retained my short hair and side parting, as did most of my friends at school, but the Summer of Love was, nevertheless, progress in another guise. New fashions, new music and art underlined the rapid and irreversible pace of change in the 1960s and made everything that went before suddenly seem very dated. It was a long decade.

So at 12, I was more concerned with unearthing, quite literally, the Storeton Tramway and chronicling the last year of steam in Wirral. Train spotting at my usual haunt near Port Sunlight station, I witnessed the rapid decline of steam that year. On some hot sunny Saturday afternoons that summer I saw steam engines travelling light from Birkenhead, sometimes coupled two or three together: they were almost certainly making their last journey to scrapyards in the Midlands or South Wales.

Occasionally I walked to Spital, the next station in the Chester direction. The first time I ventured this far was with my ever-patient friend, Michael Ainsworth. From the road the station had stone mullioned windows and a low Tudor arched entrance. We bought two singles for Bebington at the ticket counter from an older man with thinning wavy grey hair and glasses. To my delight, he invited us into his office. It was warm and cosy with an old gas cooker and aluminium tea kettle on the hob. The office window had clear glass set in mullioned windows and leaded lights that gave it the air of a church vestry. From this window we looked down on the station with its four straight platforms. Spital was a superb through mainline station that had been rebuilt in the early 1900s when the track was quadrupled. It was set in a wooded cutting with a footbridge at the southern end by the booking office. Covered steps led down to each platform and on platforms one and four there were substantial red brick waiting rooms with low hipped roofs, chimney stacks and ample canopies edged with ornate timber valences, typical of railway stations everywhere; there was a smaller brick structure without a canopy on the island platform. Looking up from the platforms, we could see the ticket office window framed by a picturesque half-timbered gable and each lamp post on the platforms carried a maroon and cream enamel sign bearing the station name.

But the station was unkempt and neglected, with an air of impending closure and dereliction. The platforms were unswept: there were drifts of leaves, litter and weeds growing through the cracks in the pavements. I said brightly to the station master that we would come back and brush the platforms and serve as volunteers to return the station to its former glory, but I don't think that either Michael or the station master were quite so keen. Although I returned to the station many times afterwards, I never did turn up with a broom.

Back at school I used this little adventure as the subject for an English essay and I suspect that it contained details about the station and particularly the interior of the ticket office that I no longer remember. Mr Colburn liked it and gave it a high mark, but then he was something of a railway enthusiast himself. In another English lesson, he announced that we would all write a poem. I found inspiration in the decline of steam and wrote a lament on the subject, which to my amazement was published in the school magazine, *The Wirralian* for 1970. It remains my one and only attempt at poetry. The very last steam locomotive that I saw on this line was also running light, at a brisk pace, southwards towards Chester: this was a large black freight locomotive (its number was 92166) on Saturday morning, 4 November 1967. That evening the last ever train to leave Birkenhead Woodside departed for Chester.

So this part of Flanders and Swan's 1963 song, 'Slow Train' came to pass and this fine Victorian terminus station, which was praised by architectural historians as one of the few really good mainline termini outside London, was closed. Suggestions that the station building could serve another purpose like Manchester Central, which was ultimately converted into an exhibition and conference centre, or Bath Green Park, which now serves as a covered market, were hastily brushed aside. Within a year of the closure, Birkenhead Woodside was demolished. This was a tragedy. I learned more about the station after reading an article in *Railway Magazine* published in March 1968 a few months before the demolition. My train spotting friend, Roy Lowry, had the magazine delivered every month and passed his copy on to me. From this I learned that the main entrance, as originally planned, consisted of an ornate canopied entrance facing the river that led into a lofty booking office with a magnificent timber vaulted roof of baronial proportions. But this was little seen by passengers as it was used as a parcels office. And I never saw it, but I remember well the station's great twin arched roof, supported by decorative cast-iron columns, its high walls relieved with blind arcading in polychrome brickwork and stone detailing. There were rose widows in the arches and overlooking the spacious concourse there was a large station clock by Joyce of Whitchurch, Shropshire.

I did not witness the demolition but when I first saw Woodside without the station I was disorientated: the buses were still there, and so was the ferry terminus, but where the great bulk of the terminus had stood on the right, in brick, iron and glass, there was now just open ground. Soon buses and cars were parked where there had once been trains for Shrewsbury,

In the late 1960s, David occasionally caught a train from Spital to Birkenhead Central via Rock Ferry. This is the overbridge dating to 1885 at Central station photographed in 1955.

A photograph of the interior of Birkenhead Woodside station, probably taken after closure, showing the decorative brick and ironwork, dating from 1878 when the station was completed.

The final stages of the demolition of the Woodside station in October 1968.

Wolverhampton and London Paddington, to various destinations in North Wales, and even trains to Bournemouth and Hastings. Rock Ferry, a mile and a half away, became the new terminus but there were no longer any long-distance trains, just the local services to Chester and Helsby, and that year the four tracks of the main line were reduced to two; four–platform stations such as Bebington and Spital were disfigured with concrete and wire mesh fences barring access to two of the platforms. It was all very depressing. And then I heard the first rumours that our windmill was threatened with demolition …

Part 4:

Ireland

11

The Emerald Isle

Aged 8 going on 9, Ireland crowded into my consciousness very quickly from early May 1964 when I learned that we were to go there for our summer holiday. Until then Ireland had been no more than a stamp in my collection. Then I learned of the Emerald Isle: apparently a term coined in the late eighteenth century by the poet William Drennan (1754–1820); once Thomas Cook inaugurated tours to Ireland in 1852, the idea of the Emerald Isle became inseparable from Irish tourism. Although I can't be sure, I probably first heard of St Patrick about this time, and of the song 'Molly Mallone':

> In Dublin's fair city
> Where the girls are so pretty
> I once met a girl named sweet Molly Malone

My dad introduced us to that one at the kitchen table. Then I learned of the association with the shamrock, the Irish harp and of leprechauns, and that Ireland was in all respects, green. I might have understood that southern Ireland was a republic and not part of the United Kingdom, which, of course, explained why the Irish stamps were different to ours. I also learned that the state airline was called Aer Lingus and it was with this Irish carrier that we were to fly from Liverpool to Dublin.

Initially, I was a little disappointed. A third holiday in Barmouth promised a repeat of the 'steam railway bliss' I had so enjoyed the previous summer. Nevertheless, I was excited by the prospect of the flight and on Monday, 20 July we made an early start, taking a black taxi, this time bound not for Birkenhead Woodside station but for Speke Airport on the south-western edge of Liverpool and close to the banks of the Mersey. In the departure lounge of the airport, which appeared to be something of a makeshift affair, I looked out at the aircraft parked by the terminal building. One ancient-looking craft was in the colours of Dan-Air and I was struck by how old-fashioned it seemed with a tail fin in three parts like a Second World War Lancaster bomber: this was an Airspeed Ambassador dating from the early 1950s. I vividly remember the din and the cloud of bluey-grey exhaust smoke that burst from the piston engines as they were started. Another small and ancient-looking aeroplane at Speke that morning was a Douglas Dakota in the orange livery of Cambrian Airways. There was also a British Eagle Viscount looking very smart in crimson red, black and white, and then we saw our aeroplane, an Aer Lingus Fokker Friendship named *Saint Finbarr*, a small aircraft in a beautiful deep emerald green and white livery with a shamrock on the tail fin. We boarded the plane and two smartly dressed air hostesses in green suits and little pillbox hats made a fuss of us three children as we tried to fasten our seat belts. Then for the first time I experienced the terrific acceleration of an aircraft taking off and also for the first time, I left the shores of England. Our destination was Arklow in County Wicklow.

We stayed at The Royal Hotel in Arklow for nine nights. This was a mod-est-sized hotel in the High Street with a grand name but almost certainly no royal connection. My recollections of that first visit to Ireland, despite some terse entries in my 1964 diary, are fragmentary. Arklow is a small sea port with two beaches, north and south, divided by the River Avoca, which flows into the Irish Sea here. One afternoon we saw a small cargo ship leave the docks from the south beach. We had tried the north beach first, but it was untidy with lots of twigs and wood scattered across the sand. One morning walking around the town, we stumbled on a blacksmith's shop. The entrance was open, and I looked around the dark and smoky interior, marvelling at the dozens of tongs and other tools suspended from hooks on the wall. I had never seen anything like this before. I thought it was incredibly old-fashioned and picturesque. I wanted to draw it but realised it would have been a very complicated subject, so cluttered was the interior. A staple item of the smith's business was the shoeing of horses. I was amazed and delighted to find that horse-drawn carts were a common part of the scene. I had only ever seen the one rag and bone man back home with a horse and cart (or flatbed wagon, perhaps) and I had not seen him since I was an infant. The typical Irish carter wore black trousers, jacket and a waistcoat with a flat cap. Some used to stand in their carts holding the reins. The carts were not in the streets to please the tourists. They were workaday vehicles owned by local carriers, carrying goods of some sort and most – if not all – the carts I saw were fitted with rubber tyres. One carter I can still picture: a gaunt, tall, thin man with a cap and an impassive expression; on the one occasion we visited the north beach, he was there, shovelling a full load of sand into his cart, I guess to be used by the building trade. Without a glance in our direction, he drove away, standing at the reins.

I was also fascinated that there were some aspects of everyday life that were similar to things at home, yet different. I quickly realised that our British coins were used alongside Irish equivalents, all of the same size and weight except for the threepence, which was a small silver-coloured coin bearing a design of a hare on the reverse. All the Irish equivalents bore a harp on one side and a mammal of some sort on the other: so the Irish half-crown displayed a horse; the florin, a dolphin; and the penny, a hen with chickens. The lettering was different and difficult to read, but nevertheless, I thought it was attractive. Letter boxes and telephone kiosks looked very similar to those at home, except they were painted mid-green and not red. So, for me aged 9, Ireland was a sort of parallel universe that was also in some respects about thirty years behind the world I knew at home. I liked it for this: it was another escape from bland suburbia.

I recall the nineteen-arch stone bridge that spanned the Avoca: Dad told me there had been a battle there in 1798, I think he mentioned Wolfe Tone. On several mornings we walked for a mile or so up the left bank of the river watching swans flying from the water and men punting in boats. The main railway line to Dublin was on an embankment over to our left again. All the trains were diesel multiple units, mostly in an attractive livery of black and orange with a strip of white, although I noticed that some of the coaches were painted a mid-green, which I guessed (correctly) was an earlier livery of the state-owned railway, *Coras Iompair Eireann*. As we walked along the river my dad – in educational mode – told me that the railway was *adjacent* to the river. Adjacent was, that day, a new word and within a day or two I think, he also introduced me to the word *incongruous*: the result is that more than fifty years on, incongruous and adjacent remain closely related in my mind. And whenever I use the word adjacent, the River Avoca is never far away.

One day – and my diary tells me it was Tuesday, 28 July 1964 – we had an excursion by taxi to Glendalough, further north and west in the same county. It was a fine day with plenty of sun but somewhere in the middle of nowhere our taxi broke down. I was sufficiently impressed to record the fact in my diary. Somehow, we were able to continue our journey – I don't recall how, but very probably in a replacement vehicle. Back on the move, we stopped at a well-known beauty spot in the Vale of Avoca called The Meeting of the Waters, where two rivers meet to form the River Avoca. It was celebrated in verse by the Irish poet and song writer, Thomas Moore (1779–1852) and his famous lines were displayed on a painted signboard by the river:

> There is not in the wide world a valley so sweet
> As that vale in whose bosom the bright waters meet

But this beautiful location where the two clear and fast flowing rivers join in a wooded valley was being ruined: nature was being replaced by concrete. The construction of a straight-sided paved walkway in the angle of the two rivers was underway. I remember being appalled to see cement mixers and construction work in progress and being heartbroken that the local council, I presumed, was intent on replacing the natural shallows of the two rivers where they met with vertical sides of concrete, cement and paving slabs. I still regard this as one of the most appalling desecrations of a place of out-standing natural beauty that I have seen anywhere. But this was the 1960s and Ireland was keen to modernise its tourist infrastructure. This interven-tion was doubtless well intentioned, but one day, I hope, may be modified or preferably, removed altogether.

We continued on our way to Glendalough, situated in a beautiful wooded valley surrounded by mountains, another notable beauty spot, and one of Ireland's most important early Christian sites based around the life and work of St Kevin. Apparently in AD 489, Kevin, who had been ordained as a bishop, came to Glendalough – meaning the glen of the two lakes – to lead the life of a hermit in a remote and desolate location. Hermits often had a hard time: not so much because they had to endure solitude but due to the difficulty they had in maintaining it. Wherever hermits went, they tended to attract attention and however much they tried to avoid company, their wish to find solitude (typically in a cave with a stone bed) was often confounded by the arrival of 'followers'. Kevin apparently managed to hold out as a hermit for seven years but by then his fame as a holy man had spread. Ultimately this was to result in the founding of a monastic settlement including a cathedral, several churches and other monuments before his death.

Aged 9, Glendalough made an enormous impression on me. I understood that this was an ancient and holy place. We first looked in on the tiny building called St Kevin's Kitchen – a low stone building with a tower that I mistakenly thought was a kitchen chimney. We walked into a roofless church and saw a giant granite cross combined with a ring or circle, which I learned was a Celtic Cross. I noted this in my diary. We saw the tall Viking round tower dating to the ninth century, which is believed to have served as a lookout, a belfry and place of refuge to protect the inhabitants from marauding Viking invaders and looters. There were many graves near the tower, some of them recent ones, which only added to the air of solemnity and sanctity of the location. We walked as far as the edge of the nearest lake – I was impressed by that too – before turning back. Looking back on that day, I saw Glendalough as a very special place, ancient and slightly magical, containing graves with ancient human bones and perhaps the ghosts of saints, monks and pilgrims. It was as much a place of pilgrimage as a tourist destination. There were nuns in grey and priests in black visiting the ruins, mixing with the tourists like ourselves but looking serious, focussed and possibly filled with awe by the sanctity they felt around them. In contrast, when I returned fifty years later, the spell had been broken. The religious atmosphere had vanished. The priests and nuns had gone and in their place were loads of noisy and brightly dressed foreign students, speaking Spanish, walking along the pathways with colourful rucksacks and mobile phones.

We ended our holiday with one night in Dublin, having travelled up by train from Arklow. We spent the afternoon in the city centre. I recall being bored stiff as my parents looked in the windows of jewellery shops admiring the rings, brooches and pendants of dull green Connemara marble set in silver. This happened to be my first ever visit to a capital city. I was yet to visit London, so I was pleased and impressed to see Nelson's Pillar in O'Connell Street. The pillar, which was not quite as tall as Nelson's Column in Trafalgar Square, was blown up two years later by militant republicans: apparently its loss was greeted with indifference by the majority of the population, although interestingly its cultural value had earlier been recognised by such prominent Irishmen as James Joyce and W.B. Yeats. We stayed in the Great Northern Hotel before flying home the next morning. This hotel was obviously formerly owned by the Great Northern Railway, which connected Dublin with Belfast. It must have been located near the railway as I could hear the noisy chug-chugging of diesel locomotives shunting or passing with freight trains well into the night. By 1964 there was no steam left on the railways of the south.

Amazed by the warmth and hospitality we had received and the easy going and relaxed tempo of Irish life, my parents resolved to return the following year. Plans were made for a two-week stay in Youghal, a seaside town in County Cork. We were due to fly out on a Cambrian Airways Viscount on 21 July 1965 and the previous evening, the airline flew an empty aircraft into Liverpool from the Isle of Man. It was almost certainly rostered for our flight to Cork the following morning. But at a little after 6 p.m., as the plane was just a matter of seconds from landing at Speke Airport, it rolled around to the right and flipped over, crashing into the roof of a factory near the airport. The two pilots were killed instantly and two employees at the factory who were still at work were also killed. The local press observed that had the crash occurred a little earlier in the day before the end of the work's afternoon shift – and had the aircraft been carrying a full complement of passengers – several hundred people could have been killed. I was aware of the crash. On that cloudy early evening I think I heard the plane pass overhead, invisible in the grey sky, for our house was on the flight path for aircraft arriving from the west. I certainly thought so and noted the crash in my diary. But the next day I don't think I made any connection between the tragedy and the fact that the plane waiting for us at Speke Airport was not a Cambrian Airways Viscount but a 'Golden Viscount' in the bright yellow fuselage strip of Channel Airways. I suspect that after the crash some urgent phone calls were made to charter a replacement aircraft for our flight to Cork. Two years later the official report on the crash noted that the final plunge might have been caused by a failure of the flaps.

We stayed in the Atlantic Hotel near the seafront. Youghal was a very historic town with several old buildings, including the arched clock gate tower straddling Main Street and an old iron cannon preserved in the grounds of the church. Then there was the town's association with Sir Walter Raleigh (1552–1618) – I was told that he had lived in the town for a while in the late sixteenth century and brought tobacco and potatoes to these isles. And I learned of the famous story that here in Youghal, his servant, seeing smoke rising from his tobacco pipe, reputedly threw a bucket of water over him thinking he was on fire. One day we visited a municipal park near the seafront and came across a recently completed statue that was, I seem to recall, dedicated to an Irishman who had taken part in the

1798 rising. He had, so the inscription stated, been 'cruelly whipped by English redcoat soldiers'. It was the first time that I realised that there had been a troubled (and tragic) past relationship between Britain and Ireland. But arguably, the installation of this new memorial in a holiday resort was out of step with the charm offensive launched by the Irish tourist authorities in Britain at the time.

These were boom years for the Irish tourist industry and in the 1960s, Britain was the largest single market. Back home, newspapers and magazines featured adverts with slogans like 'Fly Aer Lingus', and the singer and entertainer Val Doonican (1927–2015), who rose to fame in Britain in 1964, probably played a major role in conveying the image of a quaint and old-fashioned Ireland filled with picturesque and loveable rustic characters. In his Saturday night TV shows he sat in a rocking chair wearing a woollen cardigan and with a broad smile, singing songs about Paddy McGinty's Goat and Delaney's Donkey. It was to be several decades before the Celtic Donkey gave way to the Celtic Tiger. Of course, it was the Ireland of Val Doonican that I loved: friendly, easy going and old-fashioned. For this second holiday in Ireland I decided to keep a record of the number of horse-drawn vehicles I saw. By the end of our stay in Youghal I recorded in my diary that I had seen fifty horses – meaning any quadruped – donkeys, ponies and horses of all kinds – harnessed to carts and wagons.

We stopped in Cork for a night before flying home. Whilst in Youghal, my parents had befriended a family from Cork, the Campbells, who lived in a large old house in Wellington Road. The next day, 3 August, we walked around the city with three of their children, Cliff, Margaret and Ruth, who were roughly the same age as my sisters and me. Cliff took me to the main railway station at Glanmire Road. Here I was impressed by the display in the station concourse of an early Irish steam engine of 1848, with a tall chimney and painted light green. We walked down the platform to the far end of the station, where I saw a derelict mainline steam locomotive rusting away in a siding just beyond the platform end; this was the only one I ever saw in Ireland. We also wandered about the streets of the city, crossing and recrossing the River Lee, and visited the cathedral of St Finbarr's. We also followed the railway tracks around the streets of Cork. I saw several diesel-hauled freight trains lumbering slowly along these lines across the city. The next day we returned home from the airport in torrential rain. It was to be three years before we returned to Ireland.

12

The Secret Garden

Around 1967 or 1968 my parents became good friends with our new neighbours, Dave and Bet Mitchel, who had recently moved into the bungalow across the road at 2 Orchard Way. Dave was a Birkenhead policeman, a tall, dark and handsome man, probably about 35. He and his wife were always friendly and approachable. They had no children of their own and perhaps it was because of this that they gave quite a lot of time to us three children. We often went over to see them. Dave once took me to a police cricket match to help with the scoring, but they doted on my two sisters, Janet and Helen. Sometimes at weekends or on fine evenings after school, Dave would drive us to the coast at Parkgate or West Kirby for a leisurely stroll along the seafront and an ice cream.

In May 1968, around Whitsun, they took us out for the day to North Wales, to a cottage at Llanrhaeadr yn Cinmerch between Denbigh and Ruthin that was owned by one of Bet's aunts. We arrived at a whitewashed stone house in a secluded wooded location. The interior was comfortably furnished in a cottage style with dark wooden furniture and lots of ornamental brassware around. It was cosy and comfortable, and a perfect holiday home or getaway. It was a sunny day and we explored the garden, where I was intrigued to find a small free-standing structure, whitewashed and roughly circular that had neither windows nor doors. I loosened a few stones in the wall so I could peer in with the aid of a torch, although I was not able to see much. Most likely it was an old privy, but why it was sealed up was a mystery. In the afternoon we took a short walk into the neighbouring countryside, where we came across a clear, cold mountain stream in a wood. I took off my shoes and paddled in the shallow water. It was a very happy day and anticipated some of the excitement we were to experience that summer on a three-week holiday in West Cork.

Left: David, Janet
and Helen at
Llanrhaeadr, North
Wales, May 1968.

We began our holiday in mid-July with a morning flight to Dublin. Dad collected a hire car at the airport, a turquoise green Austin 40, and we began our journey. West Cork was a long way from Dublin and our destination was more than 200 miles south and west from the airport. There were no motorways in Ireland in the 1960s, no bypasses or ring roads. The journey took most of the day, driving through largely unspoiled and undulating countryside of low hills, hedgerows and green fields with occasional glimpses of distant mountains. When we reached a town, our journey invariably took us along the main street. Most of the towns were small. There was little industry to be seen and no suburbs of which to speak. Generally, we saw a church or two, shops, pubs and houses, most rendered in light grey cement and some painted a light pastel colour, typically cream or pale blue: virtually all buildings had slate roofs. We passed through Kildare, south-west of Dublin, but I remember little of the journey until we reached the small town of Cashel in County Tipperary. From a distance we could see the mass of the Rock of Cashel rising above the surrounding low-lying countryside. The rock is surmounted by an impressive and picturesque group of grey stone medieval ruins that include a cathedral and a tall slim round tower, like the one I had seen a few years earlier in Glendalough.

We continued on through Mitchelstown, where we stopped for a pub lunch of sandwiches and crisps. This was my first sight of the inside of a pub. At home, pubs were definitely out of bounds to anyone under the age of 18 but here in Ireland, where everything seemed more easy-going, children were allowed in. One pub we stopped at – and it might have been the one in Mitchelstown – doubled as the local undertaker. Helen was prone to car sickness and was placed in the middle of the rear seat, so she could look forward and in theory be less affected by the motion of the car. I always sat behind Mum and Janet on the right behind Dad driving. The following year an interruption of this routine was to have far-reaching consequences. But that day Helen was sick, inside the car. After driving through Mallow we continued our journey through Macroom and then into West Cork, passing through Dunmanway, Drimoleague and to Skibbereen. From here it was a short, final lap to our destination, Castletownshend, which we reached late afternoon.

For the next three weeks, our temporary home in Castletownshend was a self-catering flat on the ground floor of Shana Court, a large Georgian detached house on Main Street, one of the largest in the village. It had a tall hipped slate roof with two tall chimney stacks, while the exterior was rendered with rough cast cement relieved at the front with raised white horizontal bands. The sash windows were also white and there was a fan light over the front door. I guess the house probably dated to about 1750–75. We entered the property through an arched driveway on the right of the house and this led to a range of outbuildings on the right of the yard that doubtless originally served as the coach house and stable block. The courtyard continued round to the left, bounded on one side by the rear of the house and on the other two sides by high stone walls that contained two pointed-arch doorways.

We entered the house through a back door in this rear yard that led straight into a good-sized kitchen with a gas cooker, shelves for crockery, chairs and a large table. The living room was wonderful. I had never seen a room quite like this before. It was spacious and high ceilinged and looked out to the front through two long sash windows. The room contained a white marble fireplace and had dark oak polished floorboards. It was the first time I had seen floorboards like this: rich, dark and lustrous from years of polishing. The furniture was comfortable and informal and included armchairs and a sofa, a table and bureau with rugs on the floor. There was no television. A door at the far end led to the front hall, which also had a polished timber floor and a hall table with a lamp; stairs led to a first-floor flat. There was a bathroom and two bedrooms.

'All Bedrooms' said the owner's particulars, 'have interior sprung mattresses and bedside lights.' They also had 'H.& C.' basins.

The house had apparently belonged to a local doctor but was now owned by the Townshend family, who lived in the castle that fronted the small harbour. Here they ran a bed and breakfast business and let three other properties in the village as holiday homes: Speranza, a house near Shana Court, and a cottage further up Main Street that had been split into two, Virginia Cottage and Fuchsia Cottage. The Townshends were direct descendants of Colonel Richard Townsend (d. 1692) who had served in Oliver Cromwell's Irish army and had settled in Castletownshend – then known as Castletown – in about 1665. Eventually the settlement took the name of the family.

Castletownshend was like nowhere I had previously seen. It was on the coast, but this was no seaside town like Arklow, Youghal or Barmouth: it was a remote and peaceful village with a tiny harbour situated in the sheltered inlet of Castle Haven. It was a dead end, with just the one road into the village that led steeply downhill to the castle and the harbour, so there was no through traffic and, therefore, hardly any noise of any sort – apart from the cries of gulls and the cawing of crows in the trees above and behind the houses. Just how tiny a place it was became evident when within an hour or so of our arrival, the three of us – Janet, Helen and I – went out to explore our new surroundings. Shana Court was on this one road, curiously called Main Street as if there might be confusion with other roads when in fact there was just one other that was rather grandly called the Mall: this ran at right angles to Main Street. At the junction of the two roads we were amazed to find two trees growing within a raised stone circular stone wall, like a giant plant pot. I thought this was charmingly mad and eccentric and could not imagine that anything like this would be tolerated at home – even in a small village. Shana Court was situated at this junction and by the two island trees.

Shana Court, Castletownshend from the Mall in 1993, looking just as it had in 1968.

Looking up Main Street with the coach entrance to Shana Court just below the two trees. Mary Anne's is on the left. The postcard was purchased by David on 1 August 1969 in the village post office further up the street.

Walking down Main Street from Shana Court we passed a pub on the right called Mary Anne's, which was the one lively location in the village, frequented by a mix of locals and the small band of holidaymakers that very often included a few yachters who would stop in the harbour on their way along the coast. Lower down on the same side there were several small houses and cottages, and at least one of these was crumbling into decay and dereliction. At the bottom of the street there was a short and narrow lane on the left that climbed past a small octagonal tower halfway up on the right with an embattled top; at the top of this lane, steps on the right led up to the entrance of the parish church, St Barrahane's, but straight ahead at the bottom of Main Street was the harbour with a slipway into the water. To the left, a short gravel driveway led to the dignified stone front of the castle. Across the harbour we looked over to more land, to Reen, that was mostly uninhabited and barren, although it contained the ruin of a small castle or fort. The open sea was virtually out of view southwards to the far right in this sheltered spot and so the water in the harbour was generally calm. Over to our immediate right there were several old warehouses, robust rectangular structures of stone. They appeared unused and semi-derelict, and their heavy timber doors were locked. The quays were green and mossy and there was an all-pervading smell of briny seaweed. We walked from one to the next but finding our way was stopped by a rocky outcrop into the water, we returned to Main Street and this time walked along the Mall. From here, one or two twisting footpaths on the left led down to the water's edge further down the creek from the warehouses. At the end of the Mall a short path led down to a small pebbly beach in a narrow cove. With Janet and Helen watching, I skimmed flat stones on the water. We then returned to the Mall and back to Shana Court for our early evening meal.

Over the next day or two we explored the rest of the village. Walking up Main Street, we reached the Post Office situated, like Shana Court, on the right. This shop also stocked sweets and postcards, which sold for sixpence. The shop also supplied newspapers and tobacco, and I purchased a box or two of The Friendly Match, made in Dublin by Maguire and Patterson, for my small collection of matchboxes back home. This shop had an almost overpowering sugary smell of sweets. It was friendly and welcoming, and we were in and out sometimes several times a day buying sweets, postcards and stamps – not to mention the odd box of matches. Further up there were houses on either side of the road, including Virginia and Fuchsia Cottage.

There were also a couple of small pubs, or bars, with very plain frontages and a simple painted name board above a single low window: there was one either side of the road near the top and they had names like Murphy's Bar or O'Brien's Bar. They looked very basic and old-fashioned, and seemed to cater for locals and not tourists. We never dared enter them. At the top of Main Street, which had climbed for about a quarter of a mile in an unbroken straight line from the slipway, the road turned sharp right and levelled off. The houses soon petered out, although I seem to recall that there was a third small licensed bar. The road then entered open country and continued in the direction of Skibbereen, the nearest town, where my parents did most of our shopping.

Around the corner of this top section of the main street we saw a driveway on the left that led to a large house hidden from view in trees. This, I was told, was Drishane, the home of the Somervilles. One of the family, Edith Somerville (1858–1949), had co-written with her second cousin, Violet Martin (1862–1915), a series of humorous novels on Irish life in the late nineteenth century and early 1900s that apparently had raised the ire of some Irish republicans with their characterisation of simple-minded Irish rustics. At the time I knew very little about Irish nationalism and how Ireland had achieved independence, and even when I did eventually learn about the long and complicated history of trouble and strife between Britain and Ireland, I never imagined that the troubles had ever reached Castletownshend, so it was with great surprise that I learned many years later that Edith's brother, Henry Boyle Townend Somerville, a retired vice admiral in the Royal Navy, was shot in this house by the IRA in 1936, ostensibly for encouraging local men to join the Royal Navy.

Further out of the village there was the Roman Catholic church. It never struck me as unusual that in a Catholic country like Ireland, the dominant place of worship in Castletownshend was the Protestant church of St Barahanne, belonging to the Church of Ireland. This was a very pretty church of grey stone with delicately fashioned pinnacles on each corner of a square tower. It was built in 1826 and designed by James Pain (1779–1877), an English-born architect who was apprenticed to the famous Regency architect John Nash, but ultimately settled in Limerick. I often visited the church. It was always open, empty and very silent. Upon entering I was struck by the whitewashed walls of the interior and the painted ceiling, so different from the churches I knew in Wirral, which were dark and sombre inside with walls of dressed stone. But this church was light and airy, and very clean; on clear days, rays of sunlight projected dappled colours from the stained glass of the windows around the interior. It contained several memorials, including a prominent one to the Townshend family, and there was a wooden oar displayed in the porch that came from one of the lifeboats of the SS *Lusitania*, sunk by enemy action in May 1915: many of the survivors had been brought ashore around this part of the Irish coast.

With a castle occupied by descendants of a Cromwellian soldier and a Protestant church in a commanding location overlooking the harbour, Castletownshend was home to several well-to-do families of the 'old ascendancy', that is the Protestant Anglo–Irish. But aged 13 I was quite unaware of this. For me the village was quintessentially Irish: a dreamy, quiet place with a micro-climate that was almost sub-tropical through its sheltered position and proximity to the Gulf Stream. Some aspects of village life were very old-fashioned. There were several ornate cast iron water pumps painted green in the two main streets – some still worked – and our milk was delivered by a pony and trap. When we first arrived, the Townshends explained to my parents that they would need to put a large jug outside the back door for our milk delivery with a saucer or plate over it to keep off the flies. There were no milk bottles with silver foil tops. Then every morning the dairyman halted his cart in the yard and filled our jug from a large grey metal churn.

We also got to know one or two of the residents. At the foot of the little lane that led towards the church there was a long, low cottage that snuggled in a sort of level hollow, so that as we walked up the lane we looked down on it. It was occupied by an old woman with white hair and a bright apple-like face. I never went inside, although I think my sisters did and how I wished that I had! I suspect the house was very old-fashioned: I imagined there was a pot hanging over a peat fire and an old wooden Irish dresser filled with crockery, but this might have been a flight of fancy. We also got to know a kindly old man with one leg, Joe Quade, who lived in a house near the foot of Main Street on the right, near the slipway. Of course, to us three children he was always Mr Quade. He had worked over the Cork, Bandon and South Coast Railway, a long single-track line that once ran from Cork City across West Cork to Baltimore and Bantry, and had lost his leg in a work accident. The line had closed in 1961 but I seem to remember that there were bridges and other remains of the line to be seen near Skibbereen.

After a few days the three of us began to wonder what lay behind the two green doors in the courtyard. Cautiously, we tried the one nearest our back kitchen door. It was unlocked so we pushed it open and entered. We saw before us a large, heavily overgrown garden, enclosed and sheltered by high stone walls, which rose quite steeply to its furthermost boundary, where it was overhung by tall trees. The garden was to the left of the house from the front and bounded the street on the far side from the coach entrance, which was on the right. Standing inside the doorway, we were on a bottom path near the street and level with the side of the house. This path climbed by steps into the garden to our right, but at first it was impossible to make much sense of the layout, so tangled were the trees, bushes and long grass. We beat our way forward with sticks through the undergrowth until we began to make out the walls of terraces, paths and steps that had once provided the structure to a formal garden. Roughly halfway up we came to a level area of tall grass that very likely had once been a lawn; the grass was almost waist high and had dried out to the colour of straw. The top of the garden, however, was impossible to reach, so thick was the undergrowth. Along the edges of the stone path that climbed from the entrance up the side of the garden, there were large clumps of catmint, orange montbretia and other garden plants, including lots of fuchsia.

During our three weeks stay we continued to explore the garden. We beat paths through the long dried-out grass and made hollows where we could sit and hide. The garden was completely secluded and sheltered: we were sure that virtually no one else knew of its existence. It was our own secret garden and we gave it that name inspired by Frances Hodgson Burnett's famous story for children, which was a favourite of Janet's. On warm, sunny days bees and other insects buzzed and hovered over the catmint and other plants, which spread along the edges of the stone walls and paths: butterflies – peacocks, common blues and others that were new to us – fluttered from one plant to another, spreading their wings when they settled, basking in the sun; and in the tree tops behind the garden there was the sound of crows cawing in competition to the gulls in the harbour.

A day or two later, after we had fully explored our secret garden, we opened the other door from the yard and found a second walled garden. This one was easier to look across as the vegetation was mostly uniformly low and included a lot of wild onions. Like the other garden, it was a large rectangle enclosed by rubble stone walls that climbed the hill behind the house. In the right-hand bottom corner there was a derelict stone outhouse, probably once used as a potting shed and for storing garden tools; on the left-hand border nearest the overgrown formal garden, there were several old apple trees. It was clearly the old kitchen garden. We were drawn to the top wall, which faced south and was in full sun. In its right-hand corner we could see another green door in a Gothic-arched opening. There were tall trees behind the wall. And more crows. We beat our way through the undergrowth, cutting a straight diagonal path through the low undergrowth over to the right towards the doorway. When we reached the door, we found it was bolted fast. I looked around and found a half brick and, using this, I hammered back the bolt. Then I opened the door.

I looked and stared. And what I saw quite took my breath away. I'm not too sure I knew what to expect – perhaps a back alley, or more near impenetrable undergrowth – but beyond the line of trees by the wall, we looked out on a wide expanse of countryside, with cows grazing peacefully in green grass and ahead two or three small copses, tightly fenced with barbed wire, on little knolls. Cows probably always graze peacefully, but this was a particularly peaceful scene: no houses, no roads and no other people. Just me, Janet and Helen, some very content cows munching grass, and overhead the occasional caw of a crow, otherwise silence. We walked first one way and then the other, realising that we were just the other side of the back garden walls of the houses on this side of Main Street. Eventually we settled on turning right where, slightly downhill (in the direction of the harbour) we could see a wood nearby, and as we approached it we saw it was bounded on two sides by a fence of old black iron railings. In the side facing us there was an iron wicket gate. We pushed it open and entered. Through the trees and thick undergrowth, we could just about make out a straight path on a falling gradient. I led the way – Janet and Helen followed in single line – and we gingerly made our way forward, hacking and beating down brambles, nettles and overhanging branches as we went. Our progress was slow. We stepped over a tiny brook flowing from left to right and then, quite suddenly, we came up against a high old rubble stone wall with an arched tunnel entrance. The tunnel was short and lined with stone. We walked through and to our surprise found ourselves inside the base of the small octagonal tower that stands beside the lane leading to the church: the tunnel had taken us under the road.

So we knew our whereabouts and that was the end of the day's exploration. There was no way out of the tower other than the way we had come.

Over the next couple of weeks, we continued to explore the meadows behind the secret garden and the woods that plunged down steeply towards the harbour. Eventually we realised that these woods were part of the private grounds of the castle. They were thick with undergrowth, including rhododendrons, which were past flowering by July, but in the thickness of the trees we came across the ruins of another castle, very effectively camouflaged by ivy. This was an earlier structure, which I learned had been built by Colonel Richard Townsend about 1650 and was known as Bryan's Fort.

Sometimes we walked past the castle and behind the church as far up the creek as we could, wading through long meadow grass and chasing butterflies. On other days we all went by car to a nearby beach – or 'strand' as the Irish say – at Tracarta. Beyond the sheltered creek of Castle Haven, the countryside above the village was wild and windswept with low hills and rocky outcrops, large stretches of bracken and rough pasture. There were few trees or buildings of any sort. This was the setting of Tracarta, which faced out to open sea without any trappings of the 'seaside'. It could only be reached by leaving the car on a road above the beach and walking the last few hundred yards down to the shore along a rough and narrow farm track that passed a stone farmhouse. We often met the farmer by his front garden wall. He was friendly and always had something to say, but spoke in a brogue so thick and fast it could have been Gaelic: I could hardly pick out a single word but used to nod and smile and look astonished. The beach was pebbly and flanked by low cliffs and rocky promontories; a few hundred yards off the shore was Horse Island, which I believe belonged to the farmer. It was a remote and quiet stretch of coast: we often had the entire beach to ourselves, even though it was high summer. The sea was often rough and grey – and cold. This was the Atlantic Ocean: to the west, next stop: North America. I don't recall swimming in it much, but Janet was in her element: she loved the sea and seemed at home on this unspoilt, rugged stretch of coast.

We repeated the holiday the following year, four weeks this time from 14 July. Dad had recently bought his first car, a navy blue, F-reg Triumph Herald Estate, so instead of flying we crossed the Irish Sea by the overnight ferry from Liverpool to Dublin, sleeping in a cabin the size of a wardrobe. We followed last year's route from Dublin to Castletownshend, past the Rock of Cashel, through Michelstown, Mallow and Macroom, and upon arriving quickly settled into the familiar surroundings of the garden flat at Shana Court. Everything was just as we had left it the previous summer – the only change was that 'progress' had reached the village in the shape of an electric milk float in place of the pony and cart. Now our milk arrived in glass milk bottles like those at home. We renewed our acquaintance with the two walled gardens and what lay beyond – our walk to the tower, across the meadows to the top of the steep woods behind the Townsend's home, the castle. We returned to the strand at Tracarta, met the cheerful farmer again on our way down to the beach, and did our shopping several times a week in Skibbereen.

And it was in Skibbereen – about a week into the holiday – that on a flickering black and white television on the wall in a pub around the middle of the day, we witnessed one of the most momentous events of the twentieth century: the first landing on the Moon. Several months earlier, over Christmas 1968, I had followed the first ever manned flight to the Moon by the crew of Apollo 8. This was the first time anyone had seen the 'dark side' of the Moon and in colour magazines we saw the planet Earth as no one had ever seen it before, from afar, a beautiful, jewel-like blue sphere streaked with cloud. Orbiting the Moon, one of the astronauts also took another colour photograph that arguably changed how most of us saw our place in the universe: it showed the Earth rising above the lunar horizon. By comparison, the TV footage of that famous moment on 20 July when Neil Armstrong took his famous step for mankind onto the surface of the Moon was just a little disappointing. Of course, it was in black and white on black and white TV, although it would have looked no different in colour – apart, perhaps, from the red, white and blue of the US flag. The pin-sharp clarity of the colour photographs from Apollo 8 was not seen in the film footage that day and I had probably expected the lunar surface to look as it did in a *Doctor Who* story from a few years earlier when the Doctor, Patrick Troughton, had a spot of bother with Cybermen on the Moon. But this film was blurred and indistinct. Also, the two astronauts wore space suits that were so thick, and doubtless so full of equipment, they brought to mind walking refrigerators. Still it was a momentous event. I am glad that I was a part of the global audience that witnessed it, probably on the following day, in a pub in a small town in West Cork.

In Castletownshend, I felt that I had entered a completely different world from suburban Wirral: an old-fashioned village, tranquil and quiet, friendly, easy going and safe. I also met people for the first time who were very different from the people I knew at home – local villagers like Joe Quade – and

I caught a glimpse of how members of the old Irish landed class lived. I also thought that one day I would like to live in a large old house in the village with polished wooden floors, old and comfortable furniture and a sunny walled garden like Shana Court. By the late 1960s I had discovered that I had some Irish ancestry. During the summer holidays of 1968, after our first visit to Castletownshend, my parents put me on a Crossville coach at Birkenhead Woodside to spend a few days with my Great Aunt Lilias in Rhos-on-Sea. She now lived on her own following the death of her older sister, Gertrude, a few years earlier. In the sunny front room of the bungalow, she produced an old leather-bound Victorian photograph album filled with faded sepia photographs of her family: there were women in silk crinolines and men with long side whiskers sitting upright in large upholstered chairs – strangers to me, but most, if not all of them, my ancestors. She named those she could remember and told me what she knew about them; I learned that there were Irish as well as Welsh roots on my mother's side. My great aunt's grandfather (my great great grandfather) was Moses Jenkins, born in Ireland around 1826. My aunt told me their home was in Ballybofey, County Donegal. Moses had probably moved to Liverpool by the late 1840s and eventually found work as a customs officer.

His wife was Catherine Connor, and her family, said my aunt, came from Co. Meath. I later discovered that Catherine was born in Bootle, Liverpool, around 1827, but very likely her parents were Irish born.

Moses Jenkins, Fred's grandfather and David's great-great-grandfather. Born in Ireland in *c.* 1826, he had probably emigrated to Liverpool by the late 1840s. He worked as a 'Landing Waiter' for HM Customs and was living in North Hill Street, Liverpool when he died in 1886.

The two holidays in Castletownshend were a 'life changing experience' for me, although I don't think that phrase or concept was current in the 1960s. It certainly was not then part of my vocabulary. We were all very happy there. Before the holiday was over, Janet and Helen exchanged addresses with a girl they had got to know in the village and then on 12 August, we left. My parents had resolved to return for a third year, staying in Fuchsia Cottage further up Main Street, but we were never to return to Ireland again as a family.

13

Broken Glass

After breakfast we made our farewells to the Townshends and drove to Cork, where we were to spend the last night of our holiday as guests of the Campbells in Cork. It was a few years since I had seen Cliff and Ruth – they had grown up and were, I thought, just a little more reserved. I remember little of the stay except that we three slept badly. The next morning, Wednesday, 13 August, we set off for Dublin. We had a ferry to catch around 6 p.m. and were due back in Liverpool early the next morning. We stopped at Waterford for lunch and then made an afternoon break at Enniscorthy in County Wexford. We were all tired. Janet stepped in a clot of blood outside a butcher's shop and was scolded for not looking where she was going.

We continued northwards and made a short break to stretch our legs in a layby where a gate led into a field. It was about 4 p.m.. We three were a little fractious. Janet and I teased Helen by swapping places when we got back in the car: I got in first instead of Janet and took the seat behind Dad, whilst Janet entered after Helen and sat behind Mum, the reverse of our usual positions with Helen as usual in the middle. We continued on our way towards Dublin. I was reading one of those 'Check your Change' booklets, this one devoted to Victorian coinage, when suddenly I felt the car making wide swerves across the road. We were in a skid. I saw Dad frantically trying to regain control of the car, turning the steering wheel violently one way and then the other. Then – within the space of a second – I realised we were going to crash on the far side of the road. My last thought was I hoped we might hit a small sapling that would take the force of the impact. Then I passed out.

When I regained consciousness, the car was quite still (and upright) and there was an eerie, deafening silence. I drew my hand down from my head. There was blood and broken glass. I saw some men jump down a high stone retaining wall behind us. I don't remember getting out of the car but when I was free, I walked away. I saw Helen on the ground, crying and covered in cuts. I briefly noticed that the bonnet of the car, which hinged at the front, was fully up and had been forced open on impact with a largish tree that had finally stopped the car: so much for the small sapling. I was completely calm; even the sight of Helen in distress had no effect on me. I saw a field of lush soft green grass in front of me and thought I needed to lie down and rest. I was vaguely aware by now that we were not likely to make the ferry. But I remained calm, in an almost trancelike state and quite alone. I sank into the soft damp grass and soon there were two or three people by my side. They put Mum's best white Aran cardigan under my head as a makeshift pillow. I thought Mum would not be too pleased about the blood stains. I also became aware that my left shoulder hurt and I remember apologising when I asked if they could remove a blade of grass that had stuck to my tongue, which they did. I remember they were very kind. I heard Dad shouting out aloud for people to get his wife out of the car: by now we had attracted quite a crowd. But I could no longer stand up and saw nothing further of the accident scene. Eventually ambulances turned up and we were stretchered into them. I shared an ambulance with Mum and Helen. Mum was groaning. Dad, I presumed, was in the other ambulance with Janet.

We were taken to the district hospital at Gorey. It seemed more convent than hospital, with nuns providing the nursing care; at the time I did not know that it was then common for state-owned hospitals in Ireland to be run by nuns. I was stretchered to a bed in a large men's ward and rather unceremoniously tipped off the stretcher by two unsmiling nuns. I had lost my shoes by now and slid onto the bed with one sock on and the other hanging off. It was about 5 p.m.. I looked around. I was in a top corner of a large ward. There was an old man in a bed to my left. To my right there was a corridor down the length of the room and then a dreary plain apple green wall with just a small window near the top. There was also high up on the wall some kind of Roman Catholic devotional arrangement – I can't remember it in detail – perhaps there was a crucifix or a bust of the Virgin Mary, but I do remember there was a small candle burning in a glass lamp. I was very depressed by these surroundings and realised I was likely to see little else for a day or two. Dad was at the far end of the ward. I could hear his cries of pain and distress. Mum, Janet and Helen – I presumed – were in a women's ward. Gradually my ability to move in the bed lessened until it took all my effort to move my head from left to right. I could feel something hard and linty when I wrinkled my forehead, so I assumed that my head must have been bandaged, but I could not remember when. Sometime later it was visiting time and the elderly man in the adjacent bed was joined by his family and friends. To my amazement they left his bedside and surrounded mine, standing in a half circle looking at me with kindness and compassion. Some made the sign of the cross. By now I was pretty motionless. I began to be sick and at some point passed water into a glass bed bottle. My urine was black. This prompted the first attention from a doctor since my arrival. It was dark outside now. He told me that as I was passing blood there was something wrong with my kidneys and I needed to be transferred immediately to a specialist kidney hospital in Dublin. I was overjoyed. I was going to escape the depressing surroundings of this hospital with its drab, virtually windowless walls and dour-faced nuns. I was taken on a trolley over to see Dad. He didn't say much but squeezed my hand tightly. I was wheeled away and given an injection in my bottom and told to count to ten. I think I made it to five …

I woke up in the ambulance as it entered Dublin. Looking up from the stretcher, I could see street lamps and the blue light rotating through the window in the roof of the vehicle. I was taken to the Meath Hospital in Dublin 8. When I arrived, my spirits rose immediately when I saw the bright lights of the hospital entrance, a modern white interior and nurses looking busy and professional. My fascination with the past did not extend to hospitals and I was relieved and delighted to be in an up to date large hospital with friendly nurses, and not a nun in sight. They told me that our road accident had been on the evening television news and, immediately feeling a little livelier, I made a joke or two. The nurses were appalled to find that my head wound had not been dressed. So the 'lint' I had felt on my forehead earlier in the evening had not been a bandage but dried blood: no wonder the family visiting the man next to me had stared at me so sorrowfully. It seems incredible that I received so little care or treatment at the hospital in Gorey and that, in a worsening state, visiting time went ahead around me. I have wondered since why this was: perhaps it was because we were Protestant and British. In contrast, at the Meath the nurses were friendly and chatted away to me. They put stitches in the gash on the left side of my head (all my injuries were on the left) and then I was placed in a special treatment room and kept under observation through the night.

The next day I was x-rayed and told I had broken my left collarbone, that my left kidney was bruised and I had internal bleeding. I was put in a sling, washed, and removed to a single room. The next day, I was told the rest of the family would be joining me. It was about two days later that Dad was brought over to my room in a wheelchair, wearing a dressing gown. He had cracked or bruised ribs and cuts. Mum and Helen, he told me, were also now in the Meath Hospital. Helen had glass in some of her wounds but otherwise was not seriously injured but Mum had a major head wound and was only semi-conscious. But Janet was dead. Dad sobbed and told me that she had died instantly in the crash from multiple injuries. Stupidly, I said we were now a family of four. After a short stay at my bedside he was wheeled out of my room and back to his ward. I was left on my own and cried for a while. Over the next week I had two vivid dreams of Janet. In the first I saw her walking towards me on a sunny path bounded by brilliantly coloured flowers. She was smiling at me. Then either in my sleep or stirring into consciousness, I realised this was just a dream and that she was never coming back. I was having to cope for the first time in my life with the utter finality of death. In the second dream a few days later, I saw her on a wild and desolate stony shore with cliffs and grey, foaming waves – like Tracarta. She was in her usual navy blue one-piece swimsuit. She was quite alone and solitary, and quite oblivious of my presence, but she seemed happy as she always was when by the sea. It was as if this was her heaven. Now I knew she had gone.

By a tragic twist of fate, our road accident coincided with the start of the Troubles in Ulster. There was also broken glass on the streets of Derry and Belfast that day. Rioting had broken out on 12 August in the Bogside area of Derry between nationalist Catholics, fighting for an end to discrimination against Irish Catholics, and the Royal Ulster Constabulary. In support of the Bogsiders, riots quickly broke out elsewhere. Within a couple of days British troops were on the streets. The events of that week in 1969 marked the beginning of the thirty-year conflict known as the Troubles. I was given a television in my hospital room and over the next few days I saw the political crisis unfold on RTE news: there was also rioting and damage in Dublin. Later it occurred to me that on the evening of the accident the national news may have carried the story of our accident after headline news about the growing crisis in Derry and Belfast and perhaps in the same bulletin made reference to people like Bernadette Devlin, Ian Paisley and others who were to become household names in Ireland and the UK over the next few years. Sadly, the Troubles broke the spell of an easy-going, welcoming Ireland, and numbers of tourists from Britain fell sharply for several years after 1969.

We were well looked after at the Meath Hospital by very kind staff and my nurses were very indulgent, making me milky coffee every night at bedtime and then sitting on the end of my bed, where some of them had a smoke! I was almost sorry to be leaving but we returned to Liverpool by plane twelve days later. We were still very weak and frail and were met at the airport by Dave and Bet Mitchell from across the road. Mum was too ill to go home and spent another two weeks in hospital in Birkenhead. Dave had gone over to Ireland to formally identify Janet's body when we were still in hospital; they and other neighbours, friends and family arranged her funeral before we returned. On the Tuesday morning of the week following the accident, Janet was buried with her maternal grandparents, Fred and Margaret, in the graveyard of our parish church, Christ Church, in Higher Bebington. Fred had designed the headstone in 1953 when Margaret had died and his close friend, the Liverpool sculptor Herbert Tyson Smith, had carved it out of a single piece of slate. This time it was Herbert's son, Geoffrey, who carved and gilded the new inscription. Many of our neighbours and friends were at the service, including Janet's best friend from school, Janet Barr. The gravestone was reinstated later that autumn. Now the 1960s were almost over, and so, I realised later, was my childhood.

Postscript

Within a year of the accident, we had left 1 Orchard Way to start a new life in Amersham in Buckinghamshire. Within the orbit of London, this was a very different world and I was homesick for Wirral. I remember that on the day we left Merseyside by train in late September 1970, there were tears in my mother's eyes. However, Amersham had a very different atmosphere from Higher Bebington and introduced me to many new things. I soon learned that we were living in 'Metroland': the silver trains of the Met Line could be seen from the back of our house as they rattled their way to Baker Street via Rickmansworth and Harrow. So I got to know of John Betjeman, then the Poet Laureate, who wrote and narrated a highly acclaimed BBC documentary on Metroland that was first shown in 1973. Amersham was still suburbia, but this was less planned or built up than the one I had previously known. There was lots of open space, woods and country footpaths, and there was an old farmhouse, converted, at the end of our road, called Hyron's Farm. Our new address was surprisingly similar to the old one: now we were living at 12 Orchard Lane, an attractive small detached house of 1926. For the first time I saw old churches and houses built with walls of silvery-grey flint. I also marvelled at the glorious countryside of the Chilterns, with their beech woods and magnificent elm trees in the hedgerows. Tragically, within a few years all the elm trees had succumbed to Dutch elm disease, but I'm glad I saw them. We also got to know London. I remember our first visit that autumn and being overwhelmed by its size. It was nothing like the jigsaw I had of the sights of London that, because it was circular, suggested that St Paul's Cathedral was just around the corner from Westminster Abbey, but I saw Big Ben and stood outside 10 Downing Street. We walked down Oxford Street and Tottenham Court Road: my horizons were widening.

But I missed my familiar surroundings and my school friends, and the loss of Janet remained a great weight on our minds: my sisters had been inseparable, and it was clear that Helen missed her deeply. I was full of many regrets: that I hadn't shown my love more – and why did we change seats in the car just before the accident? My parents, understandably, rarely spoke of it and never talked of Ireland again. After the accident, my parents had received a letter from the first person to reach the accident scene, a man from Co. Carlow, who was on his way to his father's funeral when he saw the gap in the fence where we had left the road. He had stopped to help and comfort us, and therefore missed his family funeral service: another instance of extraordinary Irish kindness.

Two years passed before I made my first return visit to Merseyside. I stayed with some friends of my mother near Penny Lane in Liverpool for two weeks of the school summer holidays in 1972 and then a few days in Bebington with various friends, including Wynne and Michael Ainsworth. Little had changed, and I was overjoyed to be back in familiar surroundings. After that I returned frequently – and still do – and over the years many things have changed. Motorway traffic now roars along the M53 at Storeton, shattering the former peace and quiet of Wirral's green belt; a large blue motorway sign, marking an exit at Junction 4, looms over the fields. No. 1 Orchard Way has been much extended and altered. The quarry has been filled in and new houses stand close to where I once stood and stared at the chasm at my feet. Most of the shops in Village Road have gone and are now private dwellings; all but one of the shops on Teehey Lane and at the top of Town Lane have changed ownership. The range of shops is different, too: there is no electrical repair shop, no haberdashers or shoe shop. And there are no blue and cream Birkenhead buses. But in spite of all the changes, I can stand on the main road looking in the direction of Birkenhead with the spire of Christ Church ahead of me on the right and feel this is my home. I never really escaped.

This book is dedicated to the memory of

Janet Wynne Eveleigh
19 May 1957–13 August 1969

Further Reading

Alan Alsbury, *Fir-Bob Land – A Look Around Higher Bebington* (Countyvise, Birkenhead, 1999).

Helena Barrett and John Phillips, *Suburban Style, The British Home 1840– 1960* (MacDonald, London, 1987).

Alan Brack, *The Wirral* (Phillimore, Chichester, 1980).

Ralph T. Brocklebank, *Birkenhead An Illustrated History* (Breedon Books, Derby, 2003).

Ian Boumphrey, *Yesterday's Birkenhead* (Ian Boumphrey, Prenton, 2007).

Ian Boumphrey, *Birkenhead – A Pictorial History* (Phillimore, Chichester, 1995).

Burnett, *A Social History of Housing 1815–1985* (David & Charles, Newton Abbot, 1978 and Methuen, London, 2nd ed 1986).

P.A. Carson and C.R. Garner, *The Silver Screens of Wirral – A History of Cinemas in Birkenhead and Bebington* (Countyvise, Birkenhead, 1990).

Elizabeth Davey, Birkenhead a History (The History Press, Stroud, 2013).

Paul Evans, *The 1960s Home* (Shire, Oxford, 2010).

Robert Ellison, *The Wirral Peninsular* (Robert Hale, London, 1955).

David J. Eveleigh, *Town House Architecture* (Shire, Oxford, 2011).

Irene Furlong, *Irish Tourism 1880–1980* (Irish Academic Press, Dublin, 2009).

Cedric Greenwood, *Merseyside – The Indian Summer Volume 1 – Return to Woodside* (Silver Link Publishing, Kettering, 2007).

Finn Jensen, *The English Semi-detached House* (Ovolo Publishing, Huntington, 2007).

R.C. Jermy, *The Storeton Tramway* (Birkenhead Press, Birkenhead, 1981).

Mike Lister, *The Industrial Railways of Port Sunlight and Bromborough Pool* (The Oakwood Press, Oxford, 1980).

Eric Mason, *The Lancashire & Yorkshire Railway in the Twentieth Century* (Ian Allan, Shepperton: Middlesex, 1954).

R.S. McNaught, 'Access Around the Back', *Railway Magazine*, March 1968.

Peter Murphy, *The History of Wirral Grammar School for Boys 1931–1991* (Knightprint, Birkenhead, 1991).

Máire and Conor Cruise O'Brien, *Ireland a Concise History* (Thames & Hudson, London, 1972 and 1992)

Rowan Patel, *The Windmills and Watermills of Wirral* (Countyvise, Birkenhead, 2016).

Nikolaus Pevsner and Edward Hubbard, *The Buildings of England Cheshire* (Harmondsworth, Middlesex, 1971).

W.G. Rear and N. Jones, *The Llangollen Line – Ruabon to Barmouth* (Foxline Publishing, Stockport, 1990).

L.T.C. Rolt, *Green and Silver* (George, Allen & Unwin, London, 1949).

Dominic Sandbrook, *Never Had It So Good: A History of Britain from Suez to The Beatles* (Abacus, London, 2005).

Dominic Sandbrook, *White Heat: A History of Britain in the Swinging Sixties 1964–70* (Abacus, London, 2007).

Peter Somerville-Large, *The Coast of West Cork* (Appletree Press, Belfast, 1972 and 1991).

Jack Wild & Stephen Chapman, *Halifax and the Calder Valley* (Bellcode Books, Todmorden, 1998).

Christian Wolmar, *Fire & Steam How the Railways Transformed Britain* (Atlantic Books, London, 2007).